Mass Communication
Concepts & Processes

Narendra Tripathi

Reference Press
4831/24, Ansari Road,
Darya Ganj,
New Delhi-110 002.
Phone: 51563444, 23260807
Fax: 51563334
E-mail: info@essessreference.com
url: www.essessreference.com

First Published : 2006

Rs. 625/-

ISBN: 81-8405-009-7

Published By:
Reference Press
4831/24, Ansari Road,
Darya Ganj,
New Delhi-110 002.
Phone: 23260807, 51563444
Fax: 51563334
E-mail: info@essessreference.com
url: www.essessreference.com

Printed in India at:
Mehra Offset Press, New Delhi.

Contents

Preface

The media, like sports and politics, had become something to talk about. To dissect and analyse those who teach media know that these conversations are essential to the functioning of a democratic society. We also know that what moves these conversations from the realm of chatting and griping to that of effective public discourse is media education-the systematic study of media and their operation in our political and economic system, as well as their contribution to the development and maintenance of the culture that binds us together.

The pedagogical features of this book are designed to support and improve media literacy skills. It lays out the elements of media literacy, and an emphasis on media literacy is woven throughout the text. Other media literacy topics include modern methods of mass communication, evaluating news based on anonymous sources, and protecting personal privacy on the internet.

Today, no discussion of any mass medium makes sense without prior understanding of the internet. It discusses how others argue that mass communication provide a forum for true debate and expression, in which the audience is provided with valuable information. The book tries to determine how talk shows influence the viewing audience, and whether this influence is beneficial or detrimental.

Author

1

Introduction to Modern Mass Communication

THE INTERNET

The history of the Internet and the Department of Defense's Advanced Research Projects Agency (ARPA), are intimately connected. Their paths are so intertwined, that for the first 17 years of the Internet's life span (1969-1986), it was known as the ARPANET. ARPA was created by the Eisenhower administration in 1958 to promote advanced science research and development. The agencies birth was a direct result of the October 1957 launch of "Sputnik" by the Soviet Union. In the days following the launch, Eisenhower met with several top United States scientists who "told him the Russians had indeed gained impressive momentum," and that "the United States would lose its scientific and technological lead unless it mobilized." To ARPA, mobilizing meant "building a community of the best technical and scientific minds in American research" to work on projects ranging from rockets, to the growing field of computers and computer systems.

One of the brightest of the scientific minds to join ARPA was J.C.R. Licklider. Licklider was a brilliant psychologist who had become fascinated with computers and human-computer interaction. He was hired by ARPA in 1962 to look into the problems inherent in human-computer interaction in the early days of computing. The Department of Defense had invested in huge unwieldy computers, that were very difficult to maintain and operate. The main problem with these computers (and most early computers) was that they were thought of as giant calculating machines. As a result, they ran in what is known as "batch mode", where the computer used all of its resources to do large-scale calculations. The problem with running in batch mode, was it made computers difficult to program, and only allowed one user to execute one program at a time. Essentially, one user or one program was taking up 100 percent of the machines processing power. As Kate Hafner and Matthew Lyon observed:

> Batch processing was a cumbersome way of computing. For even the smallest programming task, it was necessary to have the relevant code punched onto program cards, which were then combined with `control cards' to take care of the computer's administrative functions. A computer operator fed the cards into the computer or onto magnetic tape for processing, one batch at a time. Depending on the length of the queue and the complexity of the programs and problems, the wait could be long. It was not unusual to wait a day or longer for results.

Licklider recognized the limitations of batch processing, and was in favor of a new, and at its time radical theory of computing, time sharing. In a time sharing system, many people could access a computer, each running their own programs. This was made possible by having the computer "divvy out slices of Central Processing Unit (CPU) time to all the users in a rapid, sequential manner." Licklider's interest in time sharing went beyond its obvious advantages over batch processing. He was particularly interested in the fact that time sharing systems had the ability to create a community of users who communicated and interacted with each other. This led Licklider to see the computer not as a giant calculator, but as an extender of human capabilities, most notably communication. In his 1960 paper "Man-Computer Symbiosis", Licklider laid out his hope for a new type of computer; "The hope, is that in not too many years, human brains and computing machines will be coupled ... tightly, and that the resulting partnership will think as no human brain has ever thought and process data in a way not approached by the information-handling machines we know today."

This vision of the computer as a community building communications tool, came to inspire many in the ARPA ranks, as well as students and researchers in the emerging field of computer science. While at ARPA, Licklider founded the Information Processing Techniques Office (IPTO), and set about finding and funding the best computer scientists doing work in time-sharing systems. Half jokingly he referred to this group as the "Intergalactic Computer Network." Yet this rather overstated moniker for the people whom Licklider frequently exchanged memos, embodies the spirit that would lead to the development of the Internet.

Licklider's Intergalactic Network came to "describe the potential community that he realized would emerge from the interconnection of local communities of net users that developed from time-sharing." Licklider's revolutionary ideas led ARPA away from defense oriented projects and towards "advanced research in time-sharing systems, computer graphics, and improved computer languages." Thus the theoretical and practical framework had been laid for the development of an interconnected computer network. More importantly, the computing environment that Licklider envisioned had communication and resource sharing as its central goals. Goals that can still be seen in today's Internet applications, and the way that Boston College students, faculty, and staff use them.

Robert Taylor joined ARPA in 1965, and one year later became the director of the IPTO. He had been inspired by the ideas of the departed Licklider, and now would head the development of the conceptual network that Licklider had envisioned. Taylor realized the potential benefits of networking computers to share resources, in an office at ARPA known as the terminal room. In this room were three different computers, made by three different companies, that connected to three different mainframes, running at three different locations. Making matters worse, "each had a different log-in procedure" and once connected Taylor was "forced to remember which commands belonged to which computing environment."

The computers in the terminal room were meant to allow Taylor to monitor developments being made at ARPA computing centers around the country. Yet having to remember three different log-in procedures in addition to three computer languages made this both difficult and tedious.

As a result of his problems in the terminal room, Taylor set about finding funding for a project to network the terminal computers together. Taylor argued that networking these computers would allow researchers around the country to share the resources available on each of the machines on the network.. This would be advantageous as it would cut down on the duplication of existing research and allow many users to access the networks resources without having a sophisticated computer of their own, and computers in the 1960's cost huge sums of money. Further, such a network would allow many operating systems to talk to one another, a key advantage to the Defense Department, who had several computing platforms.

Taylor's proposal was accepted, and work towards creating such a network was begun. Of key importance in Taylor's proposal is the absence of any rhetoric about the

United States' communication systems ability to withstand a nuclear attack. Their is no mention of nuclear bombs or even of the ability of the military to communicate with its remaining troops if such an event were to occur. Instead, the focus is almost entirely placed on resource sharing, a focus that has very deep connections to Licklider's fascination with time-sharing systems, and his vision of an Intergalactic Computer Network. Even in the earliest stages of the development of what would become the Internet, there is no mention of the "Nuclear Winter" scenarios posited by the popular press.

In 1960, nearly six years before Robert Taylor's idea of networking ARPA sites together, two researchers were already at work developing a system that would allow for the efficient transfer of data over a high speed communications network. Paul Baran of the Rand Corporation, and Donald Davies of the British National Physical Laboratory almost simultaneously developed "packet switching" the technology which the Internet, and many other modern day communication systems is based on.

The shred of truth to the media's portrayal of the Internet being developed as an indestructible communications system, comes directly from the research of Paul Baran. While at Rand, Baran became interested in the survivability of the United States' command and control system in the event of a nuclear war. He realized that the United States' current communication system could not withstand such an attack, and as a result, the president, or military personnel would not be able to get orders out to remaining troops. The system could not withstand a nuclear attack because there was little or no redundancy built into it.

In other words, if one part of the network was damaged, traffic routed through that node simply would not make it to its intended destination. This problem was prevalent in telephone networks, because they relied on central switching points to pass data from one area to another. Baran's solution was to build a distributed network, where all nodes had the same value as every other node, and each node was connected to neighboring nodes. This would create a high level of redundancy, and allow data to travel across several paths to reach its intended destination. Even if several of the nodes on the network were to go down, data could still be routed through alternative nodes.

Baran also realized that zipping data around on his distributed network would best be accomplished by computers. Computers would divide "each message into parts, that could flood the network with what he called `message blocks,' all racing over different paths to their destination. Upon their arrival, a receiving computer would reassemble the message bits into readable form."

Computers would also serve as nodes on this network. Each node would be a self operating computer that could route data according to tables of what other nodes were available, and what was the most efficient way to get data over the network to its destination. Baran called this "hot potato routing", and described the concept as the following:

As the term "hot potato" suggests, no sooner did a message block enter a node than it was tossed out the door again as quickly as possible. If the best outgoing path was busy - or blown to bits - the message block was automatically sent out over the next best route. If that link was busy or gone, it followed the next best route, and so forth. And if the choices ran out, the data could even be sent back to the node from which it originated.

Baran's idea was poorly received by the military, who were unwilling to fully fund the development of a test network. Despite Baran's failure to persuade the military, he had produced eleven volumes of reports detailing how such a network could be created. These reports were shelved at ARPA's IPTO office, and would soon be rediscovered.

In the same year that Paul Baran had stopped work on his project, across the Atlantic, Donald Davies was conceptualizing a similar network. Instead of focus on the redundancy of the network, Davies focused on how to break up and transmit data. The data split up to send over the network, Davies called "packets". These packets were the equivalent of what Baran had called "data blocks". Davies term won out, and the technology that he and Baran had invented became known as "packet switching". Much like Baran, Davies' ideas would go largely unnoticed for several years. However, in 1967 the hard work of both of these men would be discovered and utilized heavily in the development of ARPANET.

After Bob Taylor had been given approval to move forward with his computer networking project, he realized he would need someone brilliant to head the effort. He chose Larry Roberts, an MIT educated computer scientist who had been working on interactive computer systems at MIT's Lincoln Labs.

Roberts outlined his plans for the network at a 1967 computer conference. His idea was to create a subnetwork of Internet Message Processors (IMPs) that would handle all of the networks duties like error checking and transmitting data. To connect to the larger network, a site would link to an IMP which would take care of zipping data off to other computers on the network.

Although Roberts had settled on a structure for the network, he was still unsure of whether to use phone lines or some other method to transmit data over the network. He had been leaning towards using traditional phone connections, but only because there was no apparent alternative. Luckily for Roberts, (and for the development of the Internet that we now take for granted) a representative of Donald Davies' research team was presenting a paper on the potential of a packet-switched network. Roberts happened to attend this lecture, and immediately recognized its relevance to his project. He realized that by using a packet-switched network, he could zip data around at speeds twenty-five times faster, and with far fewer lines than he had originally planned for. From the lecture Roberts also learned of the work done by Paul Baran.

Upon returning to Washington, Roberts found and studied Baran's work. The insights he gained from Baran and Davies' packet-switching ideas, allowed him to better develop a final proposal for the creation of the ARPANET. The final draft of the proposal was completed in July, 1968 and sent out to 140 companies interested in building the IMPs. Several companies like Digital and Raytheon submitted bids, and in December of 1968, the contract to build the IMPs was given to a small contracting firm, Bolt Beranek and Newman (BBN) based out of Cambridge, Massachusetts. The technical thinking displayed by Larry Roberts and the many other computer scientists who aided in developing the IMP proposal was quite impressive, however it is the spirit behind the proposal that is of the most lasting importance. This spirit, was the belief that the computer would allow people from around the country, and even the world, to share resources and communicate with each other. In doing so, a new type of community would arise, an Intergalactic Network, that would bring people together in new and exciting ways.

J.C.R. Licklider was the first to inspire people at ARPA to view the computer as a communications device. In doing so, he ensured that the development of the ARPANET would not be dictated by the cold war paranoia that the United States' communication system would fail in the event of a nuclear war. Instead, the stated goals of the ARPANET were:

1) To develop techniques and obtain experience on interconnecting computers in such a way that a very broad class of interactions were possible and
2) To improve and increase computer research productivity through resource sharing.

In these stated goals is no mention of the doomsday scenarios that Paul Baran had developed his packet-switching ideas around. Although his work was very influential in the development of the initial ARPANET proposal, it was because of its technical advantages, not its underlying reason.

This is in stark contrast to the generally accepted media account that the ARPANET was developed for the reasons that are clearly shown to be false above. By reporting the more sensational cold war scenario, the media missed the subtle reasons for the tremendous success of the current Internet. That success can be directly attributed to J.C.R. Licklider, Bob Taylor, and Larry Roberts' commitment to building a network that would serve as resource sharing and communications tool, which is exactly what the Internet remains today.

These forward thinking notions would be embodied in the birth and development of the ARPANET, and its growth into what we today call the Internet.

Roughly one year before the start of ARPANET, graduate students from the first four host sites (UCLA, Stanford Research Institute (SRI), UC Santa Barbara, and the University of Utah) gathered in Santa Barbara for an informal meeting. They discussed the development of protocols that would allow their different computers to talk to the IMPs and to each other. The group agreed to continue meeting to work out the protocols, and became known as the Network Working Group (NWG). Heading the NWG were two graduate students from UCLA, Vinton Cerf and Steve Crocker. They realized that to keep the momentum of the group going, they would need to keep notes on their meetings. This led Crocker to write what he called a "Request for Comments" (RFC) describing the basic programming needed to allow two computers to communicate. RFC 1, dated April 1969, was more than just a simple memo, but the start of an open communication process that would allow computer scientists to discuss their ideas for standards with the entire computer science community. Because the RFC was open to others thoughts and suggestions, many people contributed their ideas for the development of protocols. "RFCs have been the principal means of open expression in the computer networking community, the accepted way of recommending, reviewing, and adopting new technical standards."

The significance of RFCs goes beyond their aid in the development of Internet protocols. The spirit of openness, community, and communication embodied in the memos would permeate the development of the ARPANET, and can still be seen in the current Internet.

E-MAIL

Central to the development of any community, is the ability its members to communicate with one another. In the case of the ARPANET, this need for communication would spawn the growth of a new communications medium, electronic mail.

E-mail had been around as early as the 1960's, when the first time sharing systems were being installed on large mainframes. The obvious limitation of early e-mail was that it could only be sent to other people who used the same machine. But with the development of the

ARPANET, and its connections to sites all around the United States and eventually the world, now a user could communicate with colleagues many thousands of miles away.

The first e-mail message sent to another computer occurred in 1972. Ray Tomlinson, a BBN engineer, wrote a simple mail program that would send messages between computers. His message was only sent to another computer at BBN, but in principle it would work on the ARPANET. Thus network e-mail was born, and it would catch on like wildfire throughout the ARPANET.

In 1973 an ARPA commissioned study found that three quarters of all traffic on the ARPANET was e-mail. "ARPANET's users had warped the computer-sharing network into a dedicated, high-speed, federally subsidized electronic post-office." This explosion in use can be explained by the simple utility of being able to communicate with associates from around the country. Further, the ARPANET community needed to constantly be communicating their ideas for new protocols and technical specifications. Although e-mail presented an ideal way to cheaply and quickly communicate networking ideas, it was also a great place to gossip and talk about interesting topics. One of the most popular early mailing lists (e-mail sent to many people simultaneously) was "SF-LOVERS," for science fiction fans.

The instant popularity of e-mail is a very significant reference point for the findings presented later in this thesis. E-mail is the most widely used Internet application among Boston College students, faculty, and staff (97.6% have used e-mail). Nearly all BC users have adopted this medium, and report being comfortable with it. The simple reason is that e-mail is easy to use, and an excellent communications tool. The utility of e-mail seemingly draws all Internet users to adopt the technology very rapidly. Another important point to take from the early history of e-mail is that it was also used for entertainment purposes. This shows that even an application developed for one purpose (communication) can be used to satisfy several other functions such as entertainment.

The lasting significance of the creation of e-mail is clearly its amazing utility as a communications medium. This has led to an explosion of e-mail use in businesses, universities, schools, homes, and just about everywhere else for that matter. In many fields, asking someone for their e-mail address is no different than asking for their phone number.

The incredible utility and potential for growth of e-mail was not missed by the creators of the ARPANET. When assessing the networks success in 1979, the IPTO ARPA Completion report noted:

The largest single surprise of the ARPANET program has been the incredible popularity and success of network mail. There is little doubt that the techniques of network mail developed in connection with the ARPANET program are going to sweep the country and drastically change the techniques used for intercommunication in the public and private spheres.

TCP/IP Protocol

In the early 1970's the success of the ARPANET led to the development of several other experimental packet switched networks. These networks operated independent of the ARPANET, and exchanged data only amongst their own nodes. This led many to wonder if it was possible to join these disparate networks together.

Solving this problem fell to Vinton Cerf. Intrigued by the problem, Cerf set about diagramming the conceptual framework needed to make internetworking possible. He realized that each network would need a gateway, a machine that could send and receive data from other networks. The gateway would have to decode incoming messages into a language understandable by the host network, and also be able to encode messages from the local host network so that other networks could understand the data. Beyond gateways, a protocol would have to be developed that would allow for the sending of messages from one network to another. The solution that Cerf came up with was the Transmission Control Protocol or TCP. In a TCP network:

> Messages would be encapsulated and decapsulated in datagrams, much as a letter is put into and taken out of an envelope, and sent as end-to-end packets. These messages would be called TCP messages, and would go through gateways which would read only the envelope so that only the receiving hosts would read the contents.

The first working display of a TCP network occurred in 1977 when Cerf connected a radio network, SATNET (a satellite network), and ARPANET. Messages traveled flawlessly from the radio network, through the ARPANET, up to the satellite network, and back down to the ARPANET. This demonstration showed that disparate networks could be tied together. If a network had a gateway computer that could speak and interpret TCP messages, then it could theoretically be connected with any other network that had a similar gateway.

By 1978 TCP split into two protocols that worked in conjunction. Part of the original TCP protocol that handled the routing of data packets was broken off into a separate Internet Protocol or IP. In the new scheme, TCP would be responsible for encoding and decoding messages, and IP would tell the messages how to get to their destination. In conjunction, the two protocols became known as TCP/IP. The development of TCP/IP, and its ability to interconnect a variety of networks would lead to the explosive growth of the "Internet" a term beginning to be used to describe the interconnection of several networks into a whole.

Usenet

The tremendous success of the ARPANET was not missed by others in the world of computers. Many in the academic and professional computing community wanted access to e-mail and other resources that ARPANET provided. However, ARPANET only connected sites that were conducting funded Department of Defense research. People at other non-connected sites began to complain that they were being left out. This need to be connected led to the development of several derivative networks that were referred to as the "Poor Man's ARPANETs."

The first of these derivative networks was Usenet. Usenet was created in 1979 by graduate students at Duke and the University of North Carolina at Chapel Hill, who wanted a way to "discuss and share experiences about Unix," an advanced computer operating system. However, Usenet soon developed into more of an electronic bulletin board, where people discussed all kinds of subjects. Each subject became known as a newsgroup, and people interested in that topic could read and post messages to the group. Groups were stored on host computers that saved peoples posts for others to read.

Today Usenet is a world-wide distributed discussion system, consisting of thousands of newsgroups pertaining to an unbelievable range of topics. "At the moment there are some 2,500 separate newsgroups, whose discussions generate about seven million words of typed commentary every day."[38] The incredible array of topics covered by Usenet allows users to satisfy several needs. For example at Boston College, students who use Usenet report using it for academic (52%) and entertainment (36%) purposes. Similar to the development of e-mail, Usenet shows that a medium developed for one purpose, can be used for many.

CSNET, BITNET, AND FIDONET

At roughly the same time that Usenet was created, several other networks began to emerge. Each network came about because people wanted to communicate and have access to electronic resources. CSNET, BITNET, and Fidonet all arose to satisfy this need.

By themselves these networks would be of little significance in the history of the Internet. However, because each of these unique networks used TCP/IP to talk to one another and the ARPANET, their growth created what we now call the Internet. "Because this growing conglomeration of networks was able to communicate using TCP/IP protocols, the collection of networks gradually came to be called the `Internet," borrowing from the first word of `Internet Protocol'."

TCP/IP became such an accepted standard that the ARPANET itself switched to it in January 1983. "After TCP/IP was installed, the network could branch anywhere; the protocols made transmission of data from one network to another a trivial task."ARPANET now served as the major backbone for traffic from other networks, and became known as the ARPA Internet. Soon the fourteen year old network that started it all, would be replaced by a much faster backbone.

NSFNET AND THE END OF ARPANET

In 1984 the National Science Foundation (NSF) proposed the creation of a very fast network to connect supercomputers and also allow "regional and university computer centers that could reach the network, to physically connect to it." This allowed several regional networks to connect to the larger Internet via the new NSFNET backbone. The NSFNET was officially up and running in 1986 with a total of 170 local area networks connected. No longer was access to the Internet limited to Defense Department contractors. Now non-funded universities and networks could have full access to the Internet and its many resources.

Two years later NSF contracted with Merit, a non-profit group of eleven Michigan universities to build a much faster national network. The new network would use T1 (1.544 megabytes per second) connections to link sixteen cities across the United States. Soon after the NSFNET upgrade, hundreds of schools, universities, and others were connecting to the NSFNET and thus also connecting to the larger Internet. NSFNET took over the role of the Internet backbone, passing data from one network to another, from the slower and much older ARPANET.

NSFNET had taken over so much of the Internet's traffic, that in 1989 ARPANET was taken out of service. In 1969 the original ARPANET had four host computers connected, in 1989 the Internet had more than 10,000 hosts connected. This staggering growth was a direct result of the TCP/IP protocol developed by Vinton Cerf and funded by ARPA, not to mention the very idea of networking computers that ARPANET had spawned. Yet more than TCP/IP was at work in the growth of the Internet. Perhaps the most important factor was that people needed and wanted to communicate. Once people saw the speed and ease with which they could send messages, everybody wanted to get connected. Not only did e-mail and Usenet allow users to discuss computer science, but it also gave them the opportunity to discuss their entertainment interests. Thus the Internet became as much a social network as it was a technological one.

The World Wide Web

The year that the ARPANET died, was also the year that an entirely new medium was proposed. In March 1989, Tim Berners-Lee of the European Particle Physics Laboratory (abbreviated as CERN due to its French name), proposed the development of a distributed hypermedia system that would become known as the World Wide Web. In the ensuing years, the web would give millions of people a new way to access the Internet, and would spur the explosive growth that the network is still experiencing today.

Berners-Lee's World Wide Web proposal was in response to CERN's problem of loosing information. CERN scientists came from all over the world, and would conduct research at the lab for a year or two. When they left, their research would often be lost among the large amount of other research being conducted. Berners Lee sums this problem up below:

A problem, however, is the high turnover of people. When two years is typical of length of stay, information is constantly being lost. The introduction of the new people demands a fair amount of their time and that of others before they have any idea of what goes on. The technical details of past projects are sometimes lost forever, or only recovered after a detective investigation in an emergency. Often the information has been recorded, it just cannot be. found.

To solve this problem Berners-Lee wanted to create a system where, "There is a potential large benefit from the integration of a variety of systems, in a way which allows a user to follow links pointing from one piece of information to another one." These pieces of information would be "linked together in a way that one can go from one concept to another to find the information one wants." Taken together these associated links would be called webs, thus the name World Wide Web for an international network of associated webs.

Berners-Lee made his ideas a reality in 1990 with the development of the Hypertext Transfer Protocol (HTTP), which takes advantage of the Internet to allow for the exchange of documents regardless of location or platform. To view this information he developed a simple line mode browser that allowed users to read the text of documents and follow hypertext links to other documents. In March 1991, the HTTP protocol was implemented at CERN and the World Wide Web had officially begun. In 1992, the HTTP protocol along with the CERN browser were made available to the public, and by the end of 1993, over 500 web servers were in operation throughout the world.

This incredible growth can be largely attributed to the creation of the Mosaic web browser by Mark Anderson in February 1993. This browser allowed users to view both text and graphics, and to follow hypertext links by clicking a mouse on the desired link. This ease of use led more and more people to use the web, and in turn, more and more people and organizations placed information on it.

Largely due to the fact that the web was developed at an academic institution, the web experienced its original growth in the educational world. Hundreds of research centers, colleges, and universities began making their information available via the web. This fact is key to understanding why many Boston College faculty and students report using the web as a research tool. Eventually the business sector realized the potential of the web, and today the number of business and entertainment sites, far outdistances educational ones.

As of January 1997, there were over 640,000 Web servers, and more than fifty million Web pages. This is compared to only 500 web servers just four years ago. During the same time period, the Internet as a whole has exploded in size, largely due to the tremendous success of the World Wide Web. In 1992 the Internet had one million hosts connected. As of July 1996, that figure has jumped to twelve million hosts. Further, the Internet continues to double in size approximately every 12-15 months.

The creation of the World Wide Web made accessing the Internet far easier. The simple point and click nature of web browsers like Mosaic, and the now popular Netscape have opened up a new world of information that companies and educators have capitalized on. The web is fast growing into a mass medium, with millions of people accessing it each day.

2

Modern Media Environment

For thousands of years the complex symbolic code known as language has allowed humans to share thoughts with one another. Even before written language, humankind communicated orally and pictorially, through paintings on cave walls, for example. Communication--including state news, sports reports, and gossip--helped hold the Roman Empire together for five hundred years. Communication can also help hold a marriage or community together as well. As modern technology is radically transforming the reach and speed and methods by which individuals and organizations communicate, it is useful to inquire whether this new global web can be used to hold communities together or whether it is serving the needs of modern day empires exclusively.

We use technology every day to inform and to be informed. We watch television or listen to the radio for entertainment and for information. We talk and listen to people across town or around the world using the telephone. Increasingly we send and receive faxes, use e-mail, and use electronic bulletin-board systems or commercial network services. Some of us may even use video conferencing systems or correspond with others using electronic mail that contains graphics or video clips.

Humankind's thirst for communication and information is seemingly unquenchable, and technology is playing an increasing role. The speed by which these new technologies are advancing should cause many of us to pause and ponder some fundamental questions about new communications technology. The means with which we communicate and the policies that guide their use may not be as neutral or as beneficent as we think. Besides allowing us to share our thoughts, our media systems may be shaping them.

The commonplace nature of familiar modes of communication prevents us from looking at them objectively and, often, from thinking about them at all. The simplest question we can ask about them is "What does the technology allow us to do?" In other words, when the technology is operating correctly, "What do we use it for?" In the case of the telephone in its conventional use, two people communicate with each other synchronously using sounds--usually voice.

A television, on the other hand allows people in one location to watch and listen to moving pictures and sound that are broadcast from a different location. The converse of the previous question, "What doesn't it allow?" is rarely asked, although it's a very useful question to consider. We can't smile at a person whom we're talking with on the telephone, for example, and expect to receive a smile in return. And although the rare television program allows viewers to telephone in to a live show to express an opinion or ask a question, television is generally used for broadcasting, and viewers are never participants in any real way. People have been known to talk back, yell, or, even, shoot their television set, but these attempts at feedback fall on deaf ears. Television is a one-way street.

Although we're not accustomed to thinking along these lines, technological systems (and modern mass-media systems are certainly technological systems) affect us in many ways. Don Norman writing in Things That Make Us Smart describes this phenomenon quite clearly:

> Technology is not neutral. Each technology has properties--affordances--that make it easier to do some activities, harder to do others: The easier ones get done, the harder ones neglected. Each has constraints, preconditions, and side effects that impose requirements and changes on the things with which it interacts, be they other technology, people, or human society at large. Finally, each technology poses a mind-set, a way of thinking about it and the activities to which it is relevant, a mind-set that soon pervades those touched by it, often unwillingly. The more successful and widespread the technology, the greater its impact upon the patterns of those who use it, and consequently, the greater impact upon all of society. Technology is not neutral; it dominates.

Although Norman describes constraints imposed by the technology itself, the actual technology is just one aspect of mass-media communications systems we generally take for granted. To understand the system as a whole it is necessary to examine political, social, and economic aspects as well as the technological aspects. In this light, much of the irrelevance, vulgarity, commercialism, and lack of balance of the mass media can be viewed as a natural by-product of the pattern of near monopoly ownership and commercial dominance. While the prospect offered by community networks for overturning corporate dominance is small, it may be possible to develop alternative media systems that are community-oriented, open, accessible, and democratic that co-exist--however precariously--with the traditional closed media systems.

Influence of Television

The birth of mass communication systems has made radical changes in our consciousness that we're just beginning to contemplate. As the prospectus from the Cultural Environment (CEM) explains, "For the first time in human history, most children are born into homes where most of the stories do not come from their parents, schools, churches, communities, and in many places, not even from their native countries, but from a handful of conglomerates who have something to sell" .

This passage notes the relatively recent appropriation and overwhelming control of cultural symbols and messages by what former University of California at San Diego Professor Herbert Schiller calls the "global cultural factories." University of Pennsylvania professor George Gerbner, the founder and chair of the Cultural Environment Movement organization has conducted extensive research that reveals how far the effects of media extend. For one thing, the constant barrage of television, print ads, and billboards has helped to stamp product mottos, jingles, and images in our consciousness. Ninety percent of all U.S. six-year-olds, for example, can identify the Joe Camel character and most 10- year-olds can name more beer brands than U.S. presidents.

Gerbner has been studying the effects of television on our collective consciousness for over 25 years. At the core of his research is exhaustive analysis of thousands of prime time television shows involving tens of thousands of characters; his analysis revealed patterns that are wildly inconsistent with reality. The incidence of crime and violence, for example, is 55 times more likely to occur on television than in real life, while elderly people, a rapidly growing and powerful age group in the United States, are shown infrequently and in stereotypical roles that are often silly, impotent, or irrelevant.

That television helps to promulgate these views throughout society is strongly implied by Gerbner's research. In one experiment, Gerbner and his assistants devised a multiple-choice questionnaire designed to learn how close the world view of the test-taker matched actual real-world statistics. The conclusions were clear--and cut across all age, income, level of education, and ethnicity distinctions: The more television a person watched, the more his or her world view matched the phony world view that beams continuously into the minds of hundreds of millions of viewers.

Funding for Media

While some may quibble at some of Gerbner's conclusions, the actual and potential effect that the consciousness industries have on what we think about and how we think about it is staggering. Thus Gerbner recommends that we think both about what the current media is doing to us, and what the media could do, both to us and for us. He believes hat cultural policy that addresses these issues explicitly belongs on "center stage . . . where it has long been in most other democracies."

Although the idea is absent from public consideration in the United States, countries in Europe and especially in Scandinavia often levy taxes on theater admissions, videotapes, and other cultural events and artifacts which are paid into a fund that loans money for independent productions. Community computer networks would obviously be good candidates for such public funding and there would be scores of other viable candidates.

Talk of public funding along these lines is not currently fashionable. Politicians, corporate media moguls, and right-wing radio talk show hosts uniformly denounce public funding options of any type. Rejection of this option, however, virtually guarantees that global corporate fare will increasingly shape the images, symbols, and messages that people see, and as a consequence, the parameters of acceptable thinking.

New Media Movement

Many of us read, listen to, or watch the news as part of our regular schedule. While the companies and organizations that produce this news are undoubtedly proficient at what they do--gathering information from around the world, organizing and packaging it, maintaining a worldwide organization, employing advanced technology, soliciting advertisers, and presenting annual reports to stockholders or owners--it is less clear why they're doing it. The ubiquitous nature of the mass media generally prevents people from posing important questions, and the owners of mass media systems are unlikely to provide forums that could challenge their modus operandi. Nevertheless, the question should be asked: What use is the news?

Let's begin this query by looking at the product itself--the news and the system that produces it. Is the reportage accurate? Is it biased? And why is one story newsworthy while others are not? Who makes those determinations and by what criteria? And, finally, if we could redefine or reorient "information and communication"--the media--to enhance the role of the citizen and community, what would this new medium look like? To begin to answer this question, let's first examine some of the deficiencies of the existing mass media systems.

A Black Box

The first thing we notice about the mass media is that it's a "black box." A black box performs a function, but since it is black, the mechanism inside it can't be viewed and how it works remains a mystery. The media industry, exemplified by the medium of television, gathers information, determines its entertainment-worthiness, and packages it behind the scenes. News production is their business while news consumption is ours. When we consume "the news," we assume that what we see is accurate and, less obviously, that it is news. Conversely, what we don't see isn't news. These black boxes are extremely powerful, as they play a large part in defining public consciousness. And since the box is opaque, the community neither understands nor participates in the process.

Profits over Value

Commercial media has to make a profit in order to stay in business. This is, of course, an economic truism of capitalistic society. A stronger statement, but an element of conventional wisdom nonetheless, is that a company's primary--if not sole--obligation is to maximize profits. This stronger form has serious implications for an industry that in theory carries the responsibility of providing citizens with the information they need to actively participate in a democratic society. If a violent television program, for example, on the average can deliver more viewers and hence more advertising revenue than say, a science program for kids, the violent program will be aired. And since advertisers financially underwrite television programming, their influence over what gets aired will be far greater than that of community members with special communication and information needs.

Disjointed Offerings

Sometimes television stations or networks broadcast documentaries or "specials" on some vexing problem of society. The topic might be homelessness, drive-by shootings, youth violence, substandard education, or some other popular tragedy. Although these shows are often intended to entertain--rather than engage--they are generally more honest and useful than much of television's usual fare. However valid these documentaries might be, their context can only be described as arbitrary and schizophrenic. For example, a special on the short life-expectancy of homeless children might pop up on a Wednesday at 9:00 p.m., preceded by an hour of situation comedies and followed by half an hour of Wall Street news. The audience was not prepared for the show in any way and no discussion, update, or sequel followed it. It was a unique and unrelated event in history, lost in a series of other unique and unrelated events.

Finally, there is literally no use to the news. While there are sporadic exceptions, news is generally useless in that there are no reasonable ways to follow up on a story, get more information, or to become involved in some positive action.

Media Integration

When a form of medium begins to connect to community activities, it becomes integrative. Fortunately, there are many ways for television, radio, or newspapers to become better integrated and enmeshed in community and civic responsibilities, and community networks can play a strong role.

The media integration could go further than providing information, however. By using the community network's electronic forums, discussions could precede the airing of the show and be integrated into the show itself. Similarly, there could also be on-line discussions after the show, and people who appeared on the show could also be available on-line to answer questions and to facilitate discussion. In this scenario, a television show could be augmented by introducing an additional medium--that of an on-line community network system. By incorporating additional media--including newspapers, radio, and a variety of face-to-face meetings--interesting, exploratory public experiments could be implemented. These experiments have been tried in some locations: "We the People," in Wisconsin, is one example. The "Puget Soundings" project in Seattle, which combines community television, radio, and community networks, is another.

Discussion forums on computer-based systems encourage conversations in which public dialog is constructed in ways unlike that encountered with other information and communication technology. Forums--both moderated and unmoderated--are based on contributions from participants, and each contribution is captured and becomes a permanent part of the forum itself, a record that can be printed or distributed and may contain seeds upon which additional discussion is spawned.

Unmoderated computer-based discussions reject the producer-consumer model. Any potential "consumer" of information, commentary, issues, or questions in an electronic forum is a potential "producer" as well. Compare this to television news programs, where an organization numbering in the hundreds dispenses its version of news to people numbering in the tens of millions. In the United States this consumer-producer ratio has been steadily shrinking in recent years. According to Ben Bagdikian, former dean of the School of Journalism at the University of California at Berkeley, "twenty-three corporations control most of the business in daily newspapers, magazines, television, books and motion pictures."

The current Internet model seriously undermines the "information as commodity" world view. Millions of people routinely supply information--facts and opinions--into a shared and increasingly global knowledge resource. Additionally, new tools such as Mosaic, gopher, MUD software, and the like are being distributed without charge. Without direct financial reward, millions of people are making available information, services, and technology that is not only cheaper, but is often of higher quality than the commercial competitors. Whether this model will endure is a matter of speculation, however, as there are strong efforts underway to commercialize many of these services.

PUBLIC JOURNALISM MOVEMENT

In the last few years the concept of public journalism has been raised as an alternative approach that could circumvent some of the problems with current mass media. Public journalism promotes a more participatory approach to journalism in which the media acts as an agent to help citizens develop their own agenda and address their own problems. NYU journalism professor, Jay Rosen explains that "the newspaper's willingness to intervene, its concern for the resolution and not just the existence of the dispute, its determination to create discussion where none existed, its aggressive style of proactive neutrality--are all signs of a public journalism approach."

Public journalism strives to be professional and neutral while shifting the focus to solution-driven from problem-driven journalism. For example, when potentially divisive disputes arose in Charlotte, South Carolina between users of a popular city park, the journalists at the Charlotte Observer worked with community members to develop an op-ed page that carried suggestions for solutions and commentaries that reflected the points of views of all the concerned parties. People in the area credit the newspaper with averting a confrontation. The park was reopened the following weekend and a panel was initiated to study the park situation and develop new youth programs.

The Charlotte Observer also launched inquiries into some of Charlotte's systematic problems, such as the city's crime rate, which had risen to nineteenth in the country although its population ranking was thirty-fourth. The city's six-month "Taking Back Our Neighborhoods" initiative combined newspaper and radio coverage, town meetings, and efforts of neighborhood organizations to help understand Charlotte's crime problem and begin devising community solutions.

Two newspapers, the Wichita (Kansas) Eagle and the Charlotte Observer are in the forefront of the public journalism movement, but the effort is spreading to many other locations including Seattle, San Francisco, Dallas, and Boston. Many newspapers are active in election issues, in which citizens are being encouraged to develop a political agenda that suits their needs rather than the politicians'.

Although these efforts are far from being commonplace, there are indications that wide-ranging experimentation in new forms of public journalism are happening at the same time that newspapers and other information purveyors like radio stations are "reinventing" themselves. One interesting aspect of this change is that different types of media organizations often collaborate on a project--two rival newspapers, or radio and television stations and a newspaper, for example.

Newer electronic forms like e-mail and collaborations with community networks are being explored, and "old-fashioned" venues such as salons and neighborhood parties are being revived as forums for public discussion of civic issues. In Spokane, Washington, the Spokesman Review newspaper purchased pizza for 500 groups that met in local homes and backyards to discuss concerns, hopes, and suggestions for the future of the region. The newspaper published summaries of these meetings and sent the comments to elected officials.

While public journalism is just one aspect of the solution, it is an important one. But public journalism is not without disadvantages and risks. For one thing it may be costlier in some ways because preparing information for use rather than consumption takes more time and demands critical skills. Preparing graphic presentations of statistical information that help convey complex information requires artistic, mathematic, and communication expertise.

A more serious danger, however, could come from a media that adopted the mantle of neutrality and public interest while practicing flawed public journalism by presenting information based on false consensus, bias, exclusionary participation, or sloppy reporting. There is no solution to this problem except a new community that expects and demands excellence from the media.

Effects of Media Images

We've noted how unresponsive and inattentive the mass media is to community needs. Unfortunately, the situation is often much worse: In many cases the mass media actively battles against civil life and community values. Often the media will place the focus on some aspects of a situation, artificially elevating those aspects while ignoring other possibly more important aspects. When a person is murdered, especially if the person was rich or famous or the method itself was particularly gruesome or novel, the gory details are disseminated quickly and easily through the media and, more importantly, into our consciousness. This act of violence becomes central to the lives of many, and society's resources are marshaled toward its reportage, discussion, and judicial and penal ramifications.

While the details of one crime are forgotten until the next one occurs, the lingering mood is one of fear and suspicion. The incessant barrage of violence in the media has taken its toll. While crime has actually decreased somewhat in recent years in the United States, people perceive increased danger and hence experience fear and mistrust. Unfortunately, there is no analogous chain reaction or fanning out of influence accompanying the good or humane act. In the words of social critic Neil Postman, we Americans seem to prefer "amusing ourselves to death." Bad news makes good news, but good news is no news at all.

People will view graphic violence if it's made readily available. It is also known that some people in certain age groups are more likely to gravitate towards violent entertainment than do people in others. According to George Gerbner's research, the ratings of nonviolent television shows are--on the average--higher than of those violent shows and that difference increases as the amount and severity of the violence increases. But younger viewers (who are more desirable to advertisers) seem to prefer the more violent fare, and this provides the financial incentive for continued bloodletting on the screen.

Gerbner quotes the producer of the megadeath movie Die Hard 2 as stating that "violence travels well around the world." Jokes might not translate well and sexual themes can run into trouble with local censors, but violence is apparently universal. Exporting boosts the profitability of any television show and violent shows are more likely to be exported. Gerbner's findings reveal that crime/action shows comprise only 17 percent of domestically shown programs but 46 percent of the exported ones. Violent American shows can now be regularly seen throughout the world. Thus, the consciousness of non-Americans is now being altered according to unhealthy stereotypes and distorted views of reality manufactured in the cultural factories of America.

Mass Media as Diversion

Carl Jensen of Project Censored and others use the expression "junk news" for the wide variety of entertainment that goes under the guise of news. This was anticipated, of course, in 1984, George Orwell's distopian treatise on totalitarian possibilities. In 1984, the production and distribution of cultural material was based on the existence of two distinct social tiers. For party members, the ostensible citizens, the Ministry of Truth supplied "the citizens of Oceania with newspapers, films, textbooks, telescreen programs, plays, novels--with every conceivable kind of information, instruction, or entertainment, from a statue to a slogan, from a lyric poem to a biological treatise, and from a child's spelling book to a Newspeak dictionary." The party member of 1984 corresponds most closely to the intellectual and political elite whose opinions do matter and whose high positions and power make them indispensable allies in maintaining the status quo. For the rest of the people,. the masses or proletarians in 1984:

> There was a whole chain of separate departments dealing with proletarian literature, music, drama, and entertainment generally. Here were produced rubbishy newspapers, containing almost nothing except sport, crime, and astrology, sensational five-cent novelettes, films oozing with sex, and sentimental songs which were composed entirely by mechanical means on a special kind of kaleidoscope known as a versificator. There was even a whole subsection--Pornosec, it was called in Newspeak--engaged in producing the lowest kind of pornography, which was sent out in sealed packets and which no Party member, other than those who worked on it, was permitted to look at.

Although private corporations--rather than the state--orchestrate and define current "proletarian culture," the results are remarkably similar to those in 1984. Graphic violence--sometimes coupled with sexuality--is apparently the pornography of choice in present-day America. Violence and sex can provide a fleeting "sugar high" that removes the person--at least for the moment--from a life of deprivation, boredom, and lack of purpose or meaning. Unfortunately, this approach rarely offers even a glimpse of any social problem or a community response to a community problem. At the same time, it helps breed an entire class of apathetic, uninformed, and disconnected people who are singularly unprepared to deal with community problems.

While discussion is at the base of a democratic society, new forms of electronic network involving film, video, audio, and computer-manipulated images are becoming increasingly widespread. It is important to consider what effects these new media will have on society and whether they can be used to support the new community. One of the first questions to ask is: Who can participate? Words--both spoken and written--are easily produced by commoners as well as kings. The written form, moreover, is particularly amenable to replication and distribution in books, newspapers, pamphlets, and on community networks.

It should be noted that although text is in itself easily produced and replicated, the average person's access to an audience of potential readers has traditionally been severely limited. This is expressed in the adage about the freedom of the press being limited to those who could afford one. It is this barrier--the distribution barrier--that has been breached by computer-mediated communications. Electronic BBSs, Fidonet echoes, conferences on Usenet, and community networks all provide nearly unlimited forums for the free exchange of ideas using text.

Multimedia information, however, changes the equation. Each aspect of the media system--its form, content, production, distribution, and access--is changed with the increased emphasis on non-textual information in the on-line world, altering the "affordances" in various ways. The first consideration is what can be portrayed by the medium.

Postman argues persuasively that text is ideally suited for ideas and dialogue, while dynamic images are better suited for entertainment. In terms of production, multimedia artifacts such as movies or television shows have been produced for broadcast by teams of people working together with ample resources. Historically, at least, the more complicated the artifact is, the more expensive it is to produce and distribute, and the more likely it is to be a well-funded corporate effort designed for profitable mass consumption.

Multimedia technology is becoming increasingly available. Prices are dropping rapidly and tools are proliferating that make tasks such as editing video much easier. It's estimated that one in six households in the United States now owns a camcorder, an estimated 16 million having been sold. Since many households do not even own telephones, it seems unlikely that every household will be able to mount its own video productions any time soon. The availability of increasingly affordable and usable technology does mean that community centers, schools, libraries, and public access television centers could lend equipment and provide inexpensive or free training to community members of varying income levels.

Video Revolution

Availability is just one part of the picture, however. Another aspect is use. Will people use video technology for democratic and community ends? While there are some examples of that community orientation, much of the evidence suggests that today's camcorder users record "family documentation and ritualistic leisure practices, just as they did with the home movie camera and the Brown Box Brownie," according to media critic Laurie Oulette. Oulette points out that the "video revolution" was hailed as a tool for democracy in other countries such as China and Czechoslovakia, while both the professional media and the video technology producers themselves stress more prosaic use within the United States.

Lastly, there are questions of distribution and demand. While independent video producers have been active for years, their work has been largely ignored. The first problem is distribution: What good is access to the means of production if distribution fails? The other problem is demand. Although it's relatively difficult to see independent and alternative productions, they can be viewed if people are persistent in their efforts. But if the large majority of people would rather "amuse themselves to death," as Neil Postman suggests, then neither increased access nor distribution would make any difference.

3

Concepts and Processes of Mass Communication

Concepts of Mass Communication

The term "mass communication" is a term used in a variety of ways which, despite the potential for confusion, are usually clear from the context. These include reference to the activities of the mass media as a group, the use of criteria of a concept, "massiveness," to distinguish among media and their activities, and the construction of questions about communication as applied to the activities of the mass media. Significantly only the third of these uses does not take the actual process of communication for granted.

Mass communication is often used loosely to refer to the distribution of entertainment, arts, information, and messages by television, radio, newspapers, magazines, movies, recorded music, and associated media. This general use of the term is only appropriate as designating the most commonly shared features of such otherwise disparate phenomena as broadcast television, cable, video playback, theater projection, recorded song, radio talk, advertising, and the front page, editorial page, sports section, and comics page of the newspaper.

In this usage mass communication refers to the activities of the media as a whole and fail to distinguish among specific media, modes of communication, genres of text or artifact, production or reception situations, or any questions of actual communication. The only analytic purpose this use of the term serves is to distinguish mass communication from interpersonal, small-group, and other face-to-face communication situations. A second use of the term involves the various criteria of massiveness which can be brought to bear in analyses of media and mass communication situations.

These criteria may include size and differentiation of audience, anonymity, simultaneity, and the nature of influences among audience members and between the audience and the media.

Live television spectaculars of recent decades may be the epitome of mass communication. These may include such serious events as the funerals of John Fitzgerald Kennedy or Martin Luther King, Jr., and such entertainment spectaculars as the Olympic games, the Superbowl, and the Academy Awards. These transmissions are distributed simultaneously and regardless of individual or group differences to audience members numbering in several tens or even a few hundreds of millions. Outside of their own local groups, these audience members know nothing of each other. They have no real opportunities to influence the television representation of the events or the interpretation of those representations by other audience members.

By contrast the audience for most cable television channels is much smaller and more differentiated from other audience groups. The audience for newspapers, magazines, and movies is less simultaneous, again smaller and more differentiated, and there is the potential for a flow of local influences as people talk about articles and recommend movies. But compared to a letter, phone call, conversation, group discussion, or public lecture all of these media produce communication immensely more massive on every criterion.

All of the criteria used in defining mass communication are potentially confused when one is engaged in a specific research project or critical examination. The most confounding problem is encountered when determining the level of analysis. Should the concern be with a single communication event or with multiple events but a single communication channel? Should the focus be upon multiple channels but a single medium? Does the central question concern a moment in time or an era, a community, nation, or the world?

Radio provides an excellent example of the importance of these choices. Before television, network radio was the epitome of mass communication; it was national, live, available and listened to everywhere. Today it is difficult to think of radio this way because the industry no longer works in the same manner. Commercial radio stations depend on local and regional sources of advertising income. Essentially all radio stations are programmed to attract a special segment of a local or regional audience, and even when programming national entertainment materials such as popular songs, stations emphasize local events, personalities, weather, news, and traffic in their broadcast talk.

Radio is an industry characterized by specialized channels each attracting relatively small, relatively differentiated audiences. But the average home in the United States has five and half radios, more than twice the number of televisions. Cumulatively the U.S. audience for radio is just as big, undifferentiated, and anonymous as that for television. Is radio today, then, a purveyor of mass communication? It depends on whether the concern is with the industry as a whole or with the programming and audience of a particular station.

Most uses of the term "mass communication" fall into one of these first two categories, either to refer to the activities of the mass media as a whole, or to refer to the massiveness of certain kinds of communication. Both uses have in common that they take issues of communication for granted and instead place emphasis on the massiveness of the distribution system and the audience. Attention is given to what are called the mass media because they are the institutional and technological systems capable of producing mass audiences for mass distributed "communications."

Communication, then, ends up implicitly defined as a kind of object (message, text, artifact) that is reproduced and transported by these media. For some purposes this may be exactly the right definition. But it diminishes our ability to treat communication as a social accomplishment, as something people do rather than as an object that gets moved from one location to another. If communication is something people do, then it may or may not be successful, may or may not be healthy and happy. If communication means "to share" for example rather than "to transmit," then what, if anything, of importance is shared when people watch a television show.

Scholars of mass communication are often more interested in communication as a social accomplishment than they are in the media as mass distribution systems. This interest is based on an intellectual independence from both existing habits of terminology, and most importantly, from media institutions as they exist. The term mass, however it may be defined, is then treated as a qualification on the term communication, however it may be defined. Such intellectual exercises, of course, can work out in a great variety of ways, but a few examples will suffice.

At one extreme, if communication is defined so that interaction between parties is a necessary criterion, as in "communication is symbolic interaction," and mass is defined as an aggregate of non-interacting entities, then mass communication is an oxymoron and an impossibility. At the opposite extreme, if the couplet mass communication is defined as involving any symbolic behavior addressed "to whom it may concern" then choices of clothing, furniture, and appliance styles, body posture, gestures, and any other publicly observable activity may well count as mass communication.

Both of these extremes may seem like mere intellectual games but they are important precisely because their intellectuality frees them of the practical constraints under which we operate in other realms. The contribution of such intellectual games is precisely to stimulate new thinking. Perhaps pausing to consider the idea that mass communication may be an impossibility could help us to understand some of the paradoxes and incoherencies of contemporary American culture.

Consider a third example in which we use a model of communication to evaluate industry practices. Definitions of mass communication that take communication for granted and focus on the massiveness of the medium are always in danger of implicitly adopting, or certainly failing to question, the taken for granted criteria of evaluation already used in industries. In commercial television, just like any of the other commercial media, what is assumed is that it is a business. The conventions of the industry are to evaluate things in business terms. Is this television show good for business? Would increasing network news to an hour be a good business decision? Would noncommercial, educational programming for children be a successful business venture? In such an environment it is an important intervention to point out that these industries are communicators as well as businesses. As such they can and should be held to communicative standards. The public has a right to ask whether a television show is good for communication, whether an hour of network news would be a successful form of communication, whether there is a communication need for noncommercial, educational children's programming. As the terms of the questions shift, so, of course, may the answers. Becoming aware of such possibilities begins with being sensitive to the definitions of such terms as mass communication.

The elements such as poster, brochure, book, radio, TV, Internet, cinema, theatre etc. used for communication with masses are called mass communications.

Development of Mass Media

Mass communications have certain properties:

- Generally one-sided communication is valid
- They can choose the target audience
- They can reach a wide range of audience
- They may use symbols to draw attention of the wide range audience

Mass media has certain tasks in social life:

- It does an important public service by establishing the rules and policies of democracy.
- It gives opportunities to social groups that have different ideologies, philosophy and beliefs.

The term mass media was coined in the 1920s with the advent of nationwide radio networks and of mass-circulation newspapers and magazines. The mass-media audience has been viewed by some commentators as forming a mass society with special characteristics, notably atomization or lack of social connections, which render it especially susceptible to the influence of modern mass-media techniques such as advertising and propaganda.

During the 20th century, the advent of mass media was driven by technology that allowed the massive duplication of material at a low cost. Physical duplication technologies such as printing, record pressing and film duplication allowed the duplication of books, newspapers and movies at low prices to huge audiences. Television and radio allowed the electronic duplication of content for the first time.

Mass media had the economics of linear replication: a single work could make money proportional to the number of copies sold, and as volumes went up, units costs went down, increasing profit margins further. Vast fortunes were to be made in mass media.

In a democratic society, an independent media serves to educate the public/electorate about issues regarding government and corporate entities. Some consider concentration of media ownership to be the single greatest threat to democracy.

During the last decade of the 20th century, the advent of the World Wide Web marked the first era in which any individual could have a means of exposure on a scale comparable to that of mass media. For the first time, anyone with a web site can address a global audience, although serving high levels of web traffic is still expensive. It is possible that the rise of peer-to-peer technologies may have begun the process of making the cost of bandwidth manageable.

Although a vast amount of information, imagery, and commentary has been made available, it is often difficult to determine the authenticity and reliability of information contained in web pages. The invention of the internet has also allowed breaking news stories to reach around the globe within minutes. This rapid growth of instantaneous, decentralized communication is often deemed likely to greatly alter mass media and its relationship to society.

Mass media and Society

Despite being a relatively recent development, the mass media plays a crucial role in forming and reflecting public opinion. It communicates the world to individuals, and it reproduces modern society's self-image. But how much exogeneous influence does the media wield? Early critiques suggested that the media destroys the individual's capacity to act autonomously. Later empirical studies, however, suggest a more complex interaction between the media and society, with individuals actively interpreting and evaluating the media and the information it provides.

Theories of the Public Sphere

Habermas

In historical terms, the development of communications and transport is one of the driving forces behind the development of modern society. It made possible the industrial revolution and continues to be essential to the coherence of modern society.

For Jürgen Habermas, the development of mass media was a crucial factor in the transition from an absolutist regime to liberal-democratic society. He develops the notion that society became increasingly polarised into the spheres of 'public authority' on the one hand (referring to the emergence of the state and associated political activity); and the 'private' sphere on the other (which was the intimate domain of private relationships and the family).

With the invention of the printing press and the subsequent availability of newspapers and various other forms of printed literature, however, Habermas sees the emergence of an intermediate sphere which he refers to as the 'bourgeois public sphere'. Here, individuals gather together to critically discuss and evaluate contemporary issues, stimulated by the contents of the open press, in a fashion reminiscent of the Greek agora. Habermas claims that this public use of reason not only acts as a regulatory mechanism over the state, which is now highly visible, but also as a catalyst for the replacement of the absolutist regime with a liberal democratic government.

However, this sphere of public discourse is transient, and will eventually disappear as increasing state intervention blurs the boundaries between public and private. At the same time, commercialisation of the media will radically alter its characteristics, as it becomes merely a tool for political manipulation, largely dependent on satisfying advertisers, readers and information sources such as the government. This can easily lead to a chase towards the lowest common denominator. This can be justified on the grounds of the massive widening of audience compared to the pre-industrial press, but it must be remembered that what is being conveyed to the masses is radically different from what was newsworthy then.

Mass media today is about culture - but a culture selected for representation by the media. This process of the 'refeudalisation of the public sphere' will leave the public exempt from political discussions. It could be argued that a new kind of absolutism emerges as a result of an abuse of democracy.

Frankfurt School

Habermas depends to some extent on some early critiques of the media from the 'Frankfurt School', such as that of Max Horkheimer, Theodor Adorno and Herbert Marcuse, for whom the media was a 'culture industry' impacting on a sea of passive individuals, who merely absorb any information they are exposed to. The cause of this is the commodification of art and culture, which allows the possibility of "manipulation by demagogues".

The Frankfurt School, which arose as an attempt to explain the success of Nazism in Weimar Germany, sees the loss of individuality through decline of privacy as the cause of dependence on great mass organisations. The interdependence of highly specialised individuals, or what Émile Durkheim called 'organic solidarity', is seen as being succeeded by a new and barbarous homogeneity. Only a 'mechanical' cohesion is possible, dependent on similarity and standardisation. Horkheimer argued that, paradoxically, individuality was impaired by the decline in the impulse for collective action. 'As the ordinary man withdraws from participating in political affairs, society tends to revert to the law of the jungle, which crushes all vestiges of individuality.'

In this analysis the Frankfurters saw totalitarianism emerging as a result of corrupt social institutions and the decline of liberal principles. Thus Horkheimer: "Just as the slogans of rugged individualism are politically useful to large trusts in society seeking exemption from social control, so in mass culture the rhetoric of individuality, by imposing patterns for collective imitation, subverts the very principle to which it gives lip service." Adorno in The Jargon of Authenticity notes that "mass media can create an aura which makes the spectator seem to experience a non-existent actuality". Thus a mass-produced, artificial culture replaces what went before.

As in Jerry Mander's work, atomised individuals of mass society lose their souls to the phantom delights of the film, the soap opera, and the variety show. They fall into a stupor; an apathetic hypnosis Lazarsfeld was to call the 'narcotyzing dysfunction' of exposure to mass media. Individuals become 'irrational victims of false wants' - the wants which corporations have thrust upon them, and continue to thrust upon them, through both the advertising in the media (with its continual exhortation to consume) and through the individualist consumption culture it promulgates. Marcuse describes this as a process where addiction to media leads to absolute docility, and the public becomes 'enchanted and transformed into a clientele by the suppliers of popular culture.'

Davis Reisman in Lonely Crowd claims that "Glamour in politics, the packaging of the leader, the treatment of events by the mass media, substitutes for the self-interest of the inner directed man the abandonment to society of the outer directed man." In other words, the creation of the public sphere implies a fundamental change in social relations and individuals' ability to model their self-image on some projected normality.

Thus, according to the Frankfurt School, leisure has been industrialised. The production of culture had become standardised and dominated by the profit motive as in other industries. In a mass society leisure is constantly used to induce the appropriate values and motives in the public. The modern media train the young for consumption. 'Leisure had ceased to be the opposite of work, and had become a preparation for it.'

Marcuse points out the 'Bach in the kitchen' phenomenon: the fact that modern methods of reproduction have increased the quantity of music, art, and literature available to the public does not mean that culture spreads to the masses; rather that culture is destroyed in order to make entertainment. 'At its worst mass culture threatens not merely to cretinise our taste,' argues Rosenberg, 'but to brutalise our senses while paving the way to totalitarianism.' Lazarsfeld and Merton put the case succinctly: 'Economic power seems to have reduced direct exploitation and to have turned to a subtler type of psychological exploitation,' they wrote of the US in the 50s. Overt totalitarian force was increasingly obsolescent. Radio, film and television seemed even more effective than terror in producing compliance.

Marcuse notes a key part of this process is its sheer, relentless omnipresence: "The preconditioning does not start with the mass production of radio or TV [at a given point in time]. The people enter this stage as preconditioned receptacles of long standing. In this more complex view the public do no abdicate rational consideration of their interest blindly. More subtly, the whole basis of rational calculation is undermined."

Some argue that this is a highly pessimistic view of individuals' cognitive and interpretative capacities. Thompson thinks that individuals do not absorb information from the media passively. In his words:

> "Media messages are commonly discussed by individuals in the course of reception and subsequent to it ... [They] are transformed through an ongoing process of telling and retelling, interpretation and reinterpretation, commentary, laughter and criticism... By taking hold of messages and routinely incorporating them into our lives .. we are constantly shaping and reshaping our skills and stocks of knowledge, testing our feelings and tastes, and expanding the horizons of our experience."

Unlike Baudrillard and others, Thompson does not see 'mediated quasi-interaction' (the monological, mainly one-way communication of the mass media) as dominant, but rather as intermingling with traditional face-to-face interactions and mediated interactions (such as telephone conversations). Contrary to Habermas' pessimistic view, this allows both more information and discussion to come into the public domain (of mediated quasi-interaction) and more to be discussed within the private domain (since the media provides information individuals would not otherwise have access to).

There is also some empirical evidence suggesting that it is 'personal contact, not media persuasiveness' which counts. For example, Trenaman and McQuail found that 'don't knows' were less well informed than consistent voters, appearing uninterested, showing a general lack of information, and not just ignorance of particular policies or policies of one particular party. A similar view is Katz and Lazarsfeld's theory of the two-step flow of communication, based on a study of electoral practices of the citizens of Erie county, Ohio, during the 1940 presidential elections. This examined the political propaganda prevalent in the media at the time during the campaign period to see whether it plays an integral role in influencing people's voting.

The results contradict this: Lazarsfeld et al find evidence for the Weberian theory of party, and identify certain factors, such as socio-economic circumstances, religious affiliation and area of residence, which together determine political orientation. The study claims that political propaganda serves to re-affirm the individual's pre-disposed orientation rather than to influence or change one's voting behaviour.

In other words, political advertising impacts not on blank-sheet individuals but on people with existing beliefs formed over long periods of time, which they are correspondingly reluctant to change. Moreover, the people who are most exposed to the media are those who know from the outset whom they will vote for, and are therefore least likely to be influenced by propaganda. Thus it appears that the notion that the people who switch parties during the campaign are mainly the reasoned, thoughtful people convinced by the issues, is completely unfounded.

Lazarsfeld et al claim the real influence on undecided voters is the 'opinion leader', the individual whose own vote intention is secure, and who is well informed on the issues. Thus personal influence is primarily of greater importance than media influence albeit using information initially acquired through the media. This may have something to do with trust and authority: both opinion leaders and the general public will select the evidence and information which supports their view, placing greater weight on more trustworthy sources.

For the opinion-leader theory to be true, then, the general public would have to place greater trust in opinion leaders than in the media, so that the opinion leaders act as mediators between the public and the media, personalising and making authoritative the information the media provides. Thus "...the person-to-person influence reaches the ones who are more susceptible to change and serves as a bridge over which formal media of communications extend their influence."

From a psychological viewpoint, we may understand the personal influence of the opinion leaders in terms of group association: perceived as representing the group's desirable characteristics, other group members will aspire to the leaders' viewpoints in order to maintain group cohesiveness and thus indirectly self-assurance. However, the separation of group leaders from the general public is arguably an over-simplification of the process of media influences.

There are also empirical problems with many of these early surveys, with researchers often ignoring important findings which would ascribe significant influence to the media. Other studies supporting the opinion leader theory failed to distinguish between opinion leading in consumer and political behaviour. In political behaviour opinion leading tends to correlate positively with status, whereas this is not the case in consumer behaviour (breakfast cereals etc). So for political behaviour, the general conclusion that the media merely fixes (confirms) people's opinion is not supported. Hovland, using experimental psychology, found significant effects of information on longer-term behaviour and attitudes, particularly in areas where most people have little direct experience (eg politics) and have a high degree of trust in the source (eg broadcasting). It should be noted that since class has become an increasingly less good indicator of party (since the surveys of the 40s and 50s) the floating voter today is no longer the apathetic voter, but likely to be more well-informed than the consistent voter - and this mainly through the media.

Agenda-Setting Process

The commodification of the media inevitably led, through the competitive processes of capitalism, to the commercial character of the modern media industries. These have escalated into large-scale commercial concerns such as Rupert Murdoch's News Corp - Murdoch himself, of course, being a quintessentially global citizen, having changed nationality for business reasons.

The consequences and ramifications of the mass media relate not merely to the way newsworthy events are perceived (and which are reported at all), but also to a multitude of cultural influences which operate through the mass media. Thus Lang and Lang claim that "The mass media force attention to certain issues. They build up public images of political figures. They are constantly presenting objects suggesting what individuals in the mass should think about, know about, have feelings about."

The agenda-setting process is partly one which is an almost unavoidable function of the bureaucratic process involved in newsgathering by the large organisations which make up much of the mass media. For example, in order to get into the news, events have to happen in places convenient for the newsgathering agencies, come from a reliable and predictable source, and fit into journalists' framework of news values. Jean Seaton notes that

> "...journalists, who are better seen as bureaucrats than as buccaneers, begin their work from a stock of plausible, well-defined and largely unconscious assumptions. Part of their job is to translate untidy reality into neat stories with beginnings, middles and denouements. ... The values which inform the selection of news items usually reinforce conventional opinions and established authority. At the same time, a process of simplification filters out the disturbing or the unexpected. The need of the media to secure instant attention creates a strong prejudice in favour of familiar stories and themes, and a slowness of response when reality breaks the conventions."

Stuart Hall points out that because some of the media produce material which often is good, impartial, and serious, they are accorded a high degree of respect and authority. But in practice the ethic of the press and television is closely related to that of the homogeneous establishment, providing a vital support for the existing order. But independence is not "a mere cover, it is central to the way power and ideology are mediated in societies like ours." The public are bribed with good radio, television and newspapers into an acceptance of the biased, the misleading, and the status quo.

The media are not, according to this approach, crude agents of propaganda. They organise public understanding. However, the overall interpretations they provide in the long run are those which are most preferred by, and least challenging to, those with economic power. Greg Philo demonstrates this in his 1991 article, "Seeing is Believing", in which he showed that recollections of the 1984 miners' strike were strongly correlated with the media's original presentation of the event, including the perception of the picketing as largely violent (violence was rare), and the use of phrases which had appeared originally in the media of the time.

McCombs and Shaw demonstrate the agenda-setting effect at work in a study conducted in Chapel Hill, USA during the 1968 presidential elections. Having selected a representative sample of un-decided voters, they were asked to outline the key issues of the election as they perceived them. Concurrently, the mass media serving these subjects were collected and analysed as regards their content. The results showed a definite correlation between the two accounts of predominant issues. "The evidence in this study that voters tend to share the media's composite definition of what is important strongly suggests an agenda-setting function of the mass media."

The long-term consequences of this are significant in conjunction with the continuing concentration of ownership and control of the media, leading to accusations of a 'media elite' having a form of 'cultural dictatorship'. Thus the continuing debate about the influence of 'media barons' such as Conrad Black and Rupert Murdoch. For example, the UK Observer reported the Murdoch-owned Harper-Collins' refusal to publish Chris Patten's East and West, because of the former Hong Kong Governor's description of the Chinese leadership as "faceless Stalinists" possibly being damaging to Murdoch's Chinese broadcasting interests. In this case, the author was able to have the book accepted by another publisher, but this kind of censorship may point the way to the future. A related, but more insidious, form is that of self-censorship by members of the media in the interests of the owner, in the interests of their careers.

Long-term effects of Mass Media

While in the short term individuals can be expected to evaluate biased information in accordance with their existing beliefs, in the long term the cultural influence of the media on the average beliefs of individuals may be significant. This operates through a process of using the symbolic materials available to us in society and from our interaction with others to formulate a sense of self-identity (which then impinges further on our self-identity through its effects on our interaction with others and our interpretation of the symbolic materials).

New encounters and experiences mean the self-image is constantly re-constructed, and the media here is a crucial source of symbolic material of everything in the world outside the private circle: it mediates Habermas' public sphere to us, and distortions in that window on the world will impinge on how we perceive the world, how we interact in our private sphere and how we interact with the public sphere.

It is because of this that many sociologists view the media as negatively affecting the individual's autonomy. However, others have attempted to demonstrate that the media provides an invaluable source of multi-cultural information which enriches one's perception of the world (by enlarging our window of perception on the world) and of life, allows for a well-balanced opinion, and that the interpretation of symbolic interaction is largely dependent on cultural and socio-economic circumstances.

Jerry Mander, in Four Arguments for the Elimination of Television, takes the negative view. Mander argues that television has become the new transmission mechanism for cultural influences, but that because of the nature and structure of the medium, it encourages a global homogeneity of culture based on US cultural influences. He quotes as an example the introduction of television to the Northwest of Canada, populated mainly by Dene Indians and Inuit, which led to the erosion of traditional values, pastimes and occupations, and the desire of the young to learn English and acquire material possessions such as cars.

The previous mode of cultural transmission - nightly story-telling - ended almost completely with the introduction of television, destroying "a bond of love and respect between the young and the old that was critical to the survival of native culture. The old people were windows to the past and to a sense of 'Indianness'". Instead of dealing with their own problems, issues and culture, "they're watching a bunch of white people in Dallas drinking martinis while standing around their swimming pools and plotting how to steal from each other." Mander describes television as "the instrument for re-shaping our internal environments - our feelings, our thoughts, our ideas and our nervous systems - to match the re-created artificial environment that increasingly surrounds us: Commodity life; Technological passivity; Acceleration; Homogenisation."

Mander's theory is related to Jean Baudrillard's concept of 'hyperreality'. We can take the 1994 OJ Simpson trial as an example, where the reality reported on was merely the catalyst for the simulacra (images) created, which defined the trial as a global event and made the trial more than it was. Essentially, hyperreality is the concept that the media is not merely a window on to the world (as if a visiting alien were watching TV), but is itself part of the reality it describes. Hence (although additionally there is the question of navel-gazing) the media's obsession with media-created events.

It is this which lead Marshall McLuhan in the 1960s to say that "the medium is the message", and to suggest that mass media was increasingly creating a "global village". Thus, for example, there is evidence that Western media influences in Asia are the driving force behind rapid social change: "it is as if the 1960s and the 1990s were compressed together." A notable example is the recent introduction of television to Bhutan, with dramatic effects in terms of very rapid Westernization. This raises questions of 'cultural imperialism' (Schiller) - the de facto imposition, through economic and political power and through the media, of Western (and in particular US) culture.

What is crucial is the control of knowledge and the flow of information. Whether controlled by lack of easy means of dissipation, by feudal absolutism, state control of mass media or big business, the media sets an agenda based on who controls it, rather than necessarily being a kind of forum for bourgeois discussion of public issues. In certain circumstances this may be the case, but it will be the exception rather than the rule, and it is difficult to identify this kind of a forum with a particular stage in the development of the media. However, this does not exclude individuals from continuous, active interpretation and evaluation within the private sphere, with some feedback to the public sphere, through such mechanisms as letters to newspapers, polls and informal contacts with people who act within the public sphere.

Ultimately, such interpretation and evaluation can also lead to changes in behaviour, such as voting patterns or consumer behaviour, or in social attitudes, particularly in non-Western societies open to Western media, bringing Western ideas, values and culture. Individuals' interpretation and evaluation is constrained by the context the media provides - and the more homogeneous the media, and the more the media's agenda is uniform, the more individuals' ability to understand the 'big picture' by playing off alternative sources of information and alternative viewpoints is undermined. For the future, the internet - through blogs, forums, wikis etc - may play a role in reclaiming the public sphere for liberal-democratic debate.

4

Theories of Mass Communication

Agenda Setting Theory

According to Ghorparde, "agenda setting is a relational concept that specifies a transfer of salience from agenda primers (media) to agenda adopters (consumers)". Agenda setting research has shown that there is a correlation between what the media deems important and salience in the public mind. In simpler terms, agenda setting claims that what the media finds important will eventually be mirrored in what people think are important. It is important to note that the notion of agenda setting is positive association between the media and the audience. From agenda setting stems the formation of public opinions and the distribution of pros and cons of a particular issue. "Agenda-setting shifts the focus of attention away from immediate effects on attitudes and opinions to longer term effects on cognitions". The notion of agenda setting relies on the transfer of issues from the media to the public.

Origins of Agenda Setting Theory

Traditionally, agenda setting theory explores the relationship the news media has on the perceived salience of key political issues. But it is important to note that the transfer of salience between media and the public should not be limited to a single aspect of the mass communication process. McCombs and Shaw empirically tested this theory during the 1972 presidential campaign between Helms and Hunt. They wanted to try and show that the media has the ability to influence what issues people think, about even if it doesn't tell people what to think of those particular issues.

This study tested the hypothesized voting behavior of people in a specific region of North Carolina. The study used television commercials, television news, and telephone survey of registered voters. Data taken from the television commercials was measured using 15 different pre-selected issues, and the commercials were also coded as either depicting a positive or negative image of the candidate. The television news agenda was coded using the same format as the commercials. And the people who were surveyed on the phone were chosen by a random-digit-dialing technique. Whereas the commercials and the news was used to expose people to the candidates the telephone survey was used to find out what issues people found to be most important and whom they were planning on voting for. All the data that was collected was measured against the money each candidate spent on advertising.

According to McCombs and Shaw, the "transfer of salience from both news and advertising to the public mind can be demonstrated". The first step in the model shows that advertising salience contributes to salience in the public mind. The second part of the model depicts a relationship from the salience in the public mind to the behavioral outcome. This part of the model was determined by looking for possible associations between the voters' agendas and the advertising of the particular candidate. In conclusion, this study was devised as a test of the agenda-setting component of advertising. It is important to note that this theory needs to be continually tested to enhance its validity.

According to the agenda-setting theory, media set the agenda for public opinion by highlighting certain issues. Studying the way political campagings were convered in the media, Shaw and McCombs found the main effect of media to be agenda-setting, telling people not what to think, but what to think of.

— *Gatekeeping*: Control over the selection of content exercised by media

— *Priming*: Giving more importance to some content over other content

— *Framing*: Presenting content in a way as to guide its interpretation along certain forced lines.

Agenda Setting and Advertising

Advertising's main goal is to "focus consumers' attention on what values, products, brands, or attributes to think about rather than try to persuade consumers what to think of these". To date, there are many methods to test advertising's effectiveness: surveys, focus groups, charts, etc. One such method is through the use of the agenda setting function. With this method, the relationship between consumer choice and advertising can be analyzed and measured for effectiveness. This is an uncommon method so there is not a lot of research measuring the validity of the agenda setting theory.

There are some "contingent conditions" for agenda setting that affects the relationship between advertising and the consumer. First of all, the duration of exposure to a particular issue can be a factor because some things will catch on quicker than others. Secondly, geographic proximity is a factor. According to Palmgreen and Clarke, national issues as opposed to local ones are more likely to result in agenda setting taking place. Lastly, there is what type of medium is involved, which happens to be the most controversial factor. The majority of studies performed conclude that newspapers are more likely to create salience than any other medium.

Hypodermic Needle Theory

Some of the earliest thinking about media theories credited immense power to mass communication to influence its audiences. The first theory concerning the media's effect on society is known as the Magic Bullet or Hypodermic Needle Theory. This analysis includes a brief discussion of the central tenets of the theory, an example of the theory - the "War of the Worlds" broadcast that made history in the area of media thinking, a short biography of the theory's primary critic, an explanation of the People's Choice Study that uses propaganda to illustrate the most significant theoretical critique of the Magic Bullet Theory and a list of primary and secondary sources for further study.

Dating from the 1920s, this theory was the first attempt to explain how mass audiences might react to mass media. It is a crude model and suggests that audiences passively receive the information transmitted via a media text, without any attempt on their part to process or challenge the data. Don't forget that this theory was developed in an age when the mass media were still fairly new - radio and cinema were less than two decades old. Governments had just discovered the power of advertising to communicate a message, and produced propaganda to try and sway populaces to their way of thinking. This was particularly rampant in Europe during the First World War and its aftermath.

Basically, the Hypodermic Needle Model suggests that the information from a text passes into the mass consciouness of the audience unmediated, ie the experience, intelligence and opinion of an individual are not relevant to the reception of the text. This theory suggests that, as an audience, we are manipulated by the creators of media texts, and that our behaviour and thinking might be easily changed by media-makers. It assumes that the audience are passive and heterogenous. This theory is still quoted during moral panics by parents, politicians and pressure groups, and is used to explain why certain groups in society should not be exposed to certain media texts, for fear that they will watch or read sexual or violent behaviour and will then act them out themselves.

Central Tenets

Early thought about the mass media surrounded the thinking that when media audience members were isolated from one another, they were vulnerable targets easily influenced by mass media messages. The Magic Bullet Theory, which originated in the 1920's and 1930's, proposed that as an audience, we were all passive and equally susceptible to media messages. The media were thought to have the ability to shape public opinion and persuade the masses toward nearly any point of view desired by the author of that particular text. Early thinking was that messages were like magic bullets; they struck all members of the audience equally and created uniform effects among them in a very different way. This theory has also been known as the Hypodermic Needle Theory, using the metaphor as a reference to how the media are assumed to be injecting all audience members with the same message, causing a uniform thinking among them that the author of the media text intended.

Example: "War of the Worlds"

The classic example of the application of the Magic Bullet

Theory was illustrated on October 30, 1938 when Orson Welles and the newly formed Mercury Theater group broadcasted their radio edition of H.G. Wells' "War of the Worlds." On the eve of Halloween, radio programming was interupted with a "news bulletin" for the first time. What the audience heard was that martians had begun an invasion of Earth in a place called Grover's Mill, New Jersey.

It became known as the "Panic Broadcast" and changed broadcast history, social psychology, civil defense and set a standard for provacative entertainment. Approximately 12 million people in the United States heard the broadcast and about one million of those actually believed that a serious alien invasion was underway. A wave of mass hysteria disrupted households, interrupted religious services, caused traffic jams and clogged communication systems. People fled their city homes to seek shelter in more rural areas, raided grocery stores and began to ration food. The nation was in a state of chaos, and this broadcast was the cause of it. Media theorists have classified the "War of the Worlds" broadcast as the archetypal example of the Magic Bullet Theory. This is exactly how the theory worked, by injecting the message directly into the "bloodstream" of the public, attempting to create a uniform thinking. The effects of the broadcast suggested that the media could manipulate a passive and gullible public, leading theorists to believe this was one of the primary ways media authors shaped audience perception.

Two-step flow of Communication

As with most theories now applied to Advertising, the Two-step flow of communication was first identified in a field somewhat removed from communications-sociology. In 1948, Paul Lazarsfeld, Bernard Berelson, and Hazel Gaudet published *The People's Choice,* a paper analyzing the votersi decision-making processes during a 1940 presidential election campaign. The study revealed evidence suggesting that the flow of mass communication is less direct than previously supposed. Although the ability of mass media to reach a large audience, and in this case persuade individuals in one direction or another, had been a topic of much research since the 1920's, it was not until the *People's Choice* was published that society really began to understand the dynamics of the media-audience relationship. The study suggested that communication from the mass media first reaches "opinion leaders" who filter the information they gather to their associates, with whom they are influential. Previous theories assumed that media directly reached the target of the information. For the theorists, the opinion leader theory proved an interesting discovery considering the relationship between media and its target was not the focus of the research, but instead a small aspect of the study.

Lazarsfeld *et al* suggested that "ideas often flow from radio and print to the opinion leaders and from them to the less active sections of the population." People tend to be much more affected in their decision making process by face to face encounters with influential peers than by the mass media. As Weiss described, "Media content can be a determining influence.... What is rejected is any conception that construes media experiences as alone sufficient for a wide variety of effects." The other piece in the communication process is the opinion leader with which the media information is discussed. The studies by Lazarsfeld and his associates sparked interest in the exact qualities and characteristics that define the opinion leader.

The Opinion Leaders

A study by Robert Merton revealed that opinion leadership is not a general characteristic of a person, but rather limited to specific issues. Individuals who act as opinion leaders on one issue, may not be considered influentials in regard to other issues. A later study directed by Lazarsfeld and Katz further investigated the characteristics of opinion leaders. This study confirmed the earlier assertions that personal influence seems more important in decision making than media. Again, influential individuals seem constrained in their opinion leading to particular topics, non-overlapping among the individuals. The opinion leaders seem evenly distributed among the social, economical, and educational levels within their community, but very similar in these areas to those with whom they had influence.

Katz and Lazarsfeld did not identify any particular traits amongst opinion leaders that stand out. The traits that characterize each of the opinion leaders in their niche did have things in common, though. For one thing, the opinion leaders were identified as having the strongest interest in their particular niche. They hold positions within their community affording them special competence in their particular niches. They are generally gregarious, sociable individuals. Finally, they had/have contact with relevant information supplied from outside their immediate circle. Interestingly enough, Katz and Lazarsfeld observed that the opinion leaders receive a disproportionate amount of their external information from media appropriate to their niche.

Studies by Glock and Nicosia determined that opinion leaders act "as a source of social pressure toward a particular choice and as a source of social support to reinforce that choice once it has been made." Charles Glock explained that opinion leaders often develop leadership positions in their social circles. They achieve these positions based on their knowledge of situations outside their circles.

Criticisms

Although the theory of indirect flow of information from media to the target was quickly adopted, the original study performed by Lazarsfeld, Berelson, and Gaudet was not. It had a few faults. The panel method by which they attempted to better understand the influences reaching a voter was unfaulted. It very effectively allowed the researchers to notice changes in a voter's feelings almost immediately. The resulting unit of change was an objective measurement that could easily be recorded and compared. The faults lie in the manner with which the researchers addressed the flow of influences.

Since the research was not designed to specifically test the flow of influence, the experiment was decidedly lacking in explanations. The first problem concerning the findings of the study were that the data had to be collected in a random sample, but subjects in a random sample can only speak for themselves. For these reasons, each person could only say whether or not they considered his/herself an advice giver. Lazarsfeld and his associates in the 1940 election study were unable to determine the specific flow of influence. They determined there were a number of opinion leaders spread throughout the socio-economic groups; however, these leaders were not directly linked to particular groups within the socio-economic levels.

Even within studies specifically designed to determine who opinion leaders are and how they are different from the average populace, there have been problems born from experimental design. "The criticisms of the concept of opinion leaders has focused mainly on its methodological deficiencies." As Weimann suggested in his 1989 study of pervious research, much of the design problems involved determining the opinion leaders while studying the flow of information. There seemed to be too many factors to control. Despite the difficulties in qualifying the influentials, the theory of a group of individuals that filter the flow of media information has lived on.

Support

Although the empirical methods behind the two-step flow of communication were not perfect, the theory did provide a very believable explanation for information flow. The opinion leaders do not replace media, but rather guide discussions of media. Brosius explains the benefits of the opinion leader theory well in his 1996 study of agenda setting, "The opinion leaders should not be regarded as replacing the role of interpersonal networks but, in fact, as reemphasizing the role of the group and interpersonal contacts."

Lazarsfeld and his associates detailed five characteristics of personal contact that give their theory more validity:

— *Non-purposiveness/casualness:* One must have a reason for tuning into a political speech on television, but political conversations can just "pop-up". In this situation, the people are less likely to have their defenses up in preparation, they are more likely open to the conversation.

— *Flexibility to counter resistance*: In a conversation, there is always opportunity to counter any resistance. This is not so in media, a one sided form of communication.

— *Trust*: Personal contact carries more trust than media. As people interact, they are better able through observation of body language and vocal cues to judge the honesty of the person in the discussion. Newspaper and radio do not offer these cues.

— *Persuasion without conviction*: The formal media is forced to persuade or change opinions. In personal communication, sometimes friendly insistence can cause action without affecting any comprehension of the issues.

Menzel introduced another strong point in favor of the two-step flow of information theory. First, there are an abundance of information channels "choked" with all types of journals, conferences, and commercial messages. These are distracting and confusing to their target. With the barrage of information humans are flooded with daily, it is not hard to understand why someone might turn to a peer for help evaluating all of it.

Recent Studies

The true test of a theory lies in its timelessness, its ability to spark interest and provoke thought years after its introduction. The two step flow of communication theory has been able to remain relevant throughout the years. This should not be difficult to believe considering it has fueled at least the past few pages this year, forty years after its debut. There have been several recent studies that have addressed issues arising from Lazarsfeld's, Katz's, and Merton's studies from the 1940s. In two such studies Gabriel Weimann and Hans-Bernd Brosius addressed the setting of agendas as a two step flow of communication.

In Weimann's paper addressing the re-emergence of the opinion leader theory into modern day, he addresses several problems that have been overcome sparking the new interest in the old theory. The two-step flow of communication theory is difficult to witness in the field. Many researchers have attempted to design credible models for testing the theory, but with only minor success.

Brosius and Weimann set out to explain agenda setting using the basis of the two-step flow of communication theory determined by Lazarsfeld, Katz, and the many other researchers. To avoid the difficulties in studying the actual flow of communication, Weimann and Brosius separated the opinion leaders from their two-step flow of communication theory. Participants were studied against a scale to determine the "Strength of Personality".

The Brosius-Weimann study attempts to describe the individuals whose personal communication has impact on agenda setting. These individuals are the archetypal opinion leaders, who still control the flow of information. Weimann and Brosius define agenda setting as a two-step flow, wherein certain individuals (influentials) "collect, diffuse, filter, and promote the flow of information" from media to the community. The difference between these influentials and the opinion leaders, as Weimann stresses, is that these influentials are usually elitists, not spread throughout the community as the old theory suggested. Are these influentials a new breed? Or is there really a difference between influentials and opinion leaders? This, as yet, has not been addressed. Weimann and Brosius suggest the influentials are a subsection of the opinion leaders.

Applications of the Theory

To those who claim that there are no applications of a socio-political theory in advertising, exhibit A is the barrage of articles written daily on the very subject. No longer does the advertising industry doubt the existence or qualities of influentials, as they are most commonly referred to today. Instead, the discussion revolves around effectively targeting messages to reach these influentials.

For fifty years, the research organization Roper has considered the group of "influentials" important enough to track. Regularly, reports and studies are performed in an attempt to unlock the secret to reaching these influentials. Who are they? What has the term "influential" come to describe? According to Diane Crispell, these people are the "thought leaders" and "pioneer consumers". "Influentials are better educated and more affluent than the average American, but it is their interest in the world around them and their belief that they can make a difference that makes them influential."

The influentials today seem to be isolated in the upper class. They are the trend-setters. It is this group that is first to adopt new technology, and remains on the leading edge of trends. This is the group that advertising attempts to reach. Daily articles are published on maximizing the market by reaching these influentials. The idea remains that the most efficient media is word-of-mouth, and it is by reaching the influentials with other forms of media that this word-of-mouth is generated. It seems the opinion leaders of yesterday have been overlooked for the smaller subset of influentials.

Uses and Gratifications Approach and the Dependency Theory

Over the past few decades, technology has truly revolutionized our lives. Perhaps one of the biggest transformations has occurred within mass communication. Prior to the industrial revolution, society had a virtually nonexistent form of mass media. However, as life began to transform, mass communication began to grow in all aspects. With each decade within the twentieth century, edge-breaking theories were presented in relation to the communication field. Two theories that brought forth a relatively astonishing perspective to this field were the Uses and Gratifications Approach and the Dependency Theory. These theories truly revolutionized the way one characterizes mass communication.

Elihu Katz first introduced the Uses and Gratification Approach, when he came up with the notion that people use the media to their benefit. The perspective emerged in the early 1970's as Katz and his two colleagues, Jay Blumler and Michael Gurevitch continued to expand the idea. This theory was contemporary because it contradicted older views that assumed the audience was a passive group. The Uses and Gratifications Approach views the audience as active, meaning that they actively seek out specific media and content to achieve certain results or gratifications that satisfy their personal needs.

The sources of the media chosen are distinctive. As Jay Blumler points out in his book *The Use of Mass Communication*, "Studies have shown that audience gratifications can be derived from at least three distinct sources: media content, exposure to the media per se, and social context that typifies the situation of exposure to different media."It is clear that audiences spend time using the media in various ways. Whether they are killing time or using it as a social tool, each medium is unique in its purpose.

The uses and Gratifications Approach has five basic assumptions. As Katz, Blumler, and Gurevitch explain in the book *Mass Communication Research*, the first assumption is that "the audience is conceived as active." This idea focuses around the assumption that the viewers are goal oriented and attempt to achieve their goals through the media source. This directly reflects and responds to the needs of the audience member in obtaining the media source.

According to the book, the second basic assumption is that "in the mass communication process much initiative in linking need gratification and media choice lies with the audience member." This is encompassing the idea that people use the media to their advantage more often than the media uses them. The receiver determines what is going to be absorbed and does not allow the media to influence them otherwise. The individual opinion is more powerful than what the media is portraying.

The third basic assumption that *Mass Communication Research* directs us to is that "the media competes with other sources of need satisfaction."This focuses on the idea that each individual has several needs. In response to this, they have created a wide range of choices that will meet these needs. The strongest rival to media based sources include face-to-face communication. This can often help an individual cope with circumstances surrounding them most effectively. Because of this, mass communication must compete strongly with non-media related sources and help create a need for itself as well as a proper balance between the two.

The forth basic assumption that the book points out is that "many of the goals media use can be derived from data supplied by the individual audience members themselves."This idea claims that people are very aware of their motives and choices and are able to explain them verbally if necessary. There have been several studies in all parts of the world that have sampled viewers and come to conclusions about the type of media used as well as the content explored. Furthermore, it was found that audience members use these media forms to shape their own identities.

The final basic assumption taken from the book *Mass Communication Research* is that "value judgments about cultural significance of mass communication should be suspended while audience operations are explored on their own terms". The theorists believe that the audience can only determine the value of the media content. It is the individual audience members who make the decision to view the media; therefore, they place the value on it by their individual decision to view it.

These basic assumptions provide a framework for understanding the exact correlation between the media and the viewers. In addition, it provides a distinction as to how the audience is more or less active and the consequences of their involvement in the media as a whole.

When one explores the Uses and Gratifications Approach, another theory that has emerged becomes quite prevalent, The Dependency Theory. Melvin DeFleur and Sandra Ball-Rokeach first described The Dependency Theory in 1976. It was, in a sense, an extension or addition to the Uses and Gratifications Approach brought about a few years earlier. The theory is in essence an explanation of the correlating relationship between the media content, the nature of society, and the behavior of the audiences. It states that people in an urban society have become dependent on mass communication to assist them in receiving the information that they need, in order to make a variety of decisions concerning their everyday lives. As Stephen Littlejohn explains in his book *Theories of Human Communication*, "First you will become more dependent on media that meet a number of your needs than on media that provide just a few." Since each persons needs are different, what they depend on is clearly going to fluctuate. Therefore, if a person finds a medium that provides them with several functions that are central to their desires, they will be more inclined to continue to use that particular medium in the future.

In his book, Littlejohn goes on to explain, "The second source of dependency is social stability."In times of conflict, such as in war periods, society as a whole tends to become more dependent on the media for a sense of stability. Furthermore, one may see an increase in media usage when something important is coming up, such as a presidential election. These special circumstances make viewers more dependent on the media to find out what is happening in society.

The dependency theory brings forth many unique propositions and functions. As Sandra Rokeach and Melvin DeFleur explain in the book *Communication Research*, "The basic propositions of The Dependency Theory can be brought together and summarized as follows: The potential for mass media messages to achieve a broad range of cognitive, affective, and behavioral effects will be increased when media systems serve many unique, and central information functions." This again reiterates the idea that the more the medium has to offer, the more useful it will become.

The cognitive changes that the Dependency Theory bring forth are multi-fold. The media brings forth attitude formation and an impact on agenda setting. Since the theory complies with the idea that people rely on it for information determining their decisions, it clearly can help individuals develop certain attitudes regarding given subjects. In addition, it encourages them to converse about certain things. The affective nature of the media is quite distinctive. It can create many different feelings such as fear, anxiety, and happiness. The media also can promote behavior changes. This can result in an audience member doing something that they would not ordinarily do. The mass media possess these three abilities and because of that, society has become dependent on the media for virtually all it's outside resources in order to make decisions.

When analyzing any theory, one must looks towards some form of criteria to judge it by. The criteria that seems to be appropriate for the Uses and Gratifications Approach and The Dependency Theory seems to be logic, consistency, testability, and simplicity.

First, when analyzing the logical approach to both theories, they seem to pass. One can see with these theories that it is logical that individuals would choose what they want to view and can clearly gain from that. This is why we see an increase in viewers when important circumstances are happening within our country.

Second, when focusing on the consistency aspect to the theories, this area is one that is somewhat differential. Although the theories are not highly contested, they do not correspond completely with previous research. One may find it hard to believe that the media has no influence over the viewer at all. There are several circumstances within the field of advertising that suggest that people are influenced by the media. This suggests that people can be persuaded.

The testability aspect seems somewhat unreliable. The way that the theories were primarily tested were through sampling the audience viewers. The results could possibly be biased because individuals may not realize the power that the media has over them. In essence, the sampling was one sided.

Finally, when one looks at the simplicity of the theories, they seem to pass. Both of the theories are extremely easy to understand and comprehend. In addition, they link together, which helps the perception of them become more explicit.

With every theory, some criticism must be expected. Both the Uses and Gratifications Approach and The Dependency Theory are no exception to this act. One main criticism is based on the idea that the audience is completely active. It seems as though the theorists feel that there is not room for any middle ground. In many cases people turn to viewing the media as a result of habit. This factor is not mention in their theory. Other critics argue that the broader public does not effect individual decisions regarding the media. According to Ronald Rice, in his book *The New Media*, states, "Larger social purposes and effects have to do with why an individual, for the most part, reads a newspaper". This is simply stating that the reason why most people view media or read newspapers is to gain societal information.

Mass Communication has come a very long way over the last thirty years. Many different perspectives have been brought forth and analyzed in terms of effectiveness. The Uses and Gratifications Approach and The Dependency Theory were two theories that brought forth a new genre of ideas and aspects of cognition to mass communication. The mass media is an extremely complex system that responds to the foundation of these theories in media's everyday production.

Media Richness Theory

Media Richness Theory is the most influential theory of media choice in the organization and information sciences today. It was developed to examine the relationship between the content of managerial communication and media selection. Originally, MRT addressed traditional intraorganizational communication media such as facetoface and telephone. It has more recently been extended to include electronic means of communication. Past studies used the theory in a prescriptive mode assuming that media choices influenced employees' effectiveness. Markus results support this approach. More recently, studies have used the theory to describe and explain how individuals actually perceive and select media rather than the implications of these choices are for effectiveness. Thus, Media Richness Theory can help explain why senior managers choose to rely heavily on face-to-face meetings and telephone calls for sensitive or important communication and e-mail or written methods for routine communications. In 1987, Trevino, Lengel, and Daft first brought attention to three general reasons that managers choose particular media which were then used as the new foundations for MRT.

1. Ambiguity of the message content and richness of the communication medium
2. Situational determinants such as time and distance
3. Symbolic cues provided by the medium

Content Reasons

Content reasons involve ambiguity or equivocality (the latter term will be used throughout to mean both) and the richness of the medium. Media Richness Theory states that effective managers will choose different media for different situations based on task-related factors and the richness of the media. Richness, for media, is defined as the capacity to facilitate shared meaning, insight, and rapid understanding. Communications that foster shared meaning, insight, and rapid understanding are considered rich.

Original research on MRT classified two relevant influences on information processing: uncertainty and equivocality. Uncertainty is defined as the absence of information and represents the difference between the amount of information required to perform a task and the amount of information already given about the task. Managers respond to uncertainty by acquiring information and analyzing data. They do so by asking questions and obtaining answers. Periodic reports, group meetings, rules, and procedures can be used to reduce uncertainty within an organization.

Communication that is used simply to gather more information or data does not require rich media: and in fact is best supported through the use of leaner media. Highly equivocal communication, on the other hand, does require rich media. Equivocality has been defined as ambiguity and the existence of multiple and conflicting interpretations about a situation. Confusion and disagreement go hand-on and with equivocality. In equivocal situations, managers have to interpret the situation from vague cues (e.g., voice inflection and body language) and come up with a reasonable solution . Thus, richer media are seen as the most appropriate choice for reducing equivocality.

The media studied in the development of MRT were ranked in their ability to process equivocal information. The ranks were based on their ability to provide feedback, the availability of a number of cues to resolve confusion, language variety, and personal focus. Face-to-face communication was ranked the richest as it allows for rapid mutual feedback, permitting messages to be reinterpreted, clarified, and adjusted immediately.

In addition, face-to-face communication conveys emotion, uses nonverbal behavior to modify and control communication exchange, and therefore allows simultaneous communication of multiple cues. Since body language and visual cues are not found with telephone communication, it is not as rich as face-to-face communication. However, it still allows for fast feedback and the use of language content and audio cues. These factors, its personal nature, and its ability to use natural language, made it second on the richness scale. Written communication fell lowest on the scale. Feedback is slow, only textual information is conveyed, voice cues are absent, and visual cues are limited. These classifications were identified during early studies before electronic mail was introduced. Since then however, more studies have been conducted which have placed electronic mail between telephone and written communication media on the media richness scale.

Since many decision-making tasks have at least some equivocal aspect, managers frequently have to interpret vague cues and negotiate solutions. Equivocal situations are novel and nonrecurring and require hunches, discussion, and social support. Newer information systems, such as electronic mail, are not well suited to problems involving equivocality. When a medium is chosen that provides information that is needed to resolve the equivocality of a message, MRT researchers conclude that more effective communication will result.

Situational Reasons

Situational reasons effect media choices as well. Certain situational determinants constrain media choice behavior while others may expand manager? choices. Distance, expediency, structure, and role expectations can all constrain media choice. On the other hand, determinants such as availability and access to certain media are considered situational enablers. If people do not have access to electronic mail, that choice is obviously eliminated.

Two other situational determinants have been identified in previous research: geographic dispersion and job pressure. As communication technology has advanced, the importance of distance has diminished. Since capabilities such as e-mail and teleconferencing are available, face-to-face communication may not be required, allowing organizations to less save time and money. Job and time pressure can also influence media choices. Steinfield and Fulk found that managers were more likely to use the telephone when acting under time pressure, regardless of the degree of equivocality inherent in the situation. It is possible that e-mail offers managers a means to alleviate some of the time pressures they are constantly faced with.

Symbolic Reasons

Considering symbolic cues of the medium itself is also important in making media choices. Feldman and March suggest that managerial communication behavior often represents ritualistic responses to the need to appear rational, legitimate, competent, and intelligent. They offer that some managers may request more data than needed or send out professional looking reports in an attempt to show that their decision was rational and legitimate. On the other hand, face-to-face communication is more useful to symbolize caring or concern. For example, using e?ail to congratulate someone on a major promotion instead of doing so in person may convey a lack of concern. In addition, using new technologies may symbolize a high-tech scientific quality or desired image of status. Written communication on the other hand, may be used to symbolize authority.

Medium Theory

M. McLuhan challenged conventional definitions when he claimed that the medium is the message. With this claim, he stressed how channels differ, not only in terms of their content, but also in regard to how they awaken and alter thoughts and senses. He distinguished media by the cognitive processes each required. McLuhan popularized the idea that channels are a dominant force that must be understood to know how the media influence society and culture.

Medium theory focuses on the medium characteristics itself (like in media richness theory) rather than on what it conveys or how information is received. In medium theory, a medium is not simply a newspaper, the Internet, a digital camera and so forth. Rather, it is the symbolic environment of any communicative act. Media, apart from whatever content is transmitted, impact individuals and society. McLuhan's thesis is that people adapt to their environment through a certain balance or ratio of the senses, and the primary medium of the age brings out a particular sense ratio, thereby affecting perception.

Medium theory is an analytical theory with few empirical model building. Some of the methods used are: analysis of media characteristics and historical analysis of human perception.

Medium theory examines physical, psychological and social variables as the senses that are required to attend to the medium; whether the communication is bi-directional or uni-directional, how quickly messages can be disseminated, whether learning to encode and decode in the medium is difficult or simple, how many people can attend to the same message at the same moment, and so forth. Medium theorists argue that such variables influence the medium's use and its social, political, and psychological impact.

Knowledge Gap Theory

The knowledge gap theory was first proposed by Tichenor, Donohue and Olien at the University of Minnesota in the 70s. They believe that the increase of information in society is not evenly acquired by every member of scciety: people with higher socioeconomic status tend to have better ability to acquire information. This leads to a division of two groups: a group of better-educated people who know more about most things, and those with low education who know less. Lower socio-economic status (SES) people, defined partly by educational level, have little or no knowledge about public affairs issues, are disconnected from news events and important new discoveries, and usually aren't concerned about their lack of knowledge.

The knowledge gap can result in an increased gap between people of lower and higher socioeconomic status. The attempt to improve people's life with information via the mass media might not always work the way this is planned. Mass media might have the effect of increasing the difference gap between members of social classes.

Tichenor, Donohue and Olien present five reasons for justifying the knowledge gap.

1) People of higher socioeconomic status have better communication skills, education, reading, comprehending and remembering information.

2) People of higher socioeconomic status can store information more easily or remember the topic form background knowledge

3) People of higher socioeconomic status might have a more relevant social context.

4) People of higher socioeconomic status are better in selective exposure, acceptance and retention.

5) The nature of the mass media itself is that it is geared toward persons of higher socioeconomic status.

Media presenting information should realize that people of higher socioeconomic status get their information in a different way than lower educated people. Furthermore, this hypothesis of the knowledge gap might help in understanding the increased gap between people of higher socioeconomic status and people of lower socioeconomic status. It can be used in various circumstances.

The knowledge gap was used in a research for presidential campaigns. The knowledge gap hypothesis holds that when new information enters a social system via a mass media campaign, it is likely to exacerbate underlying inequalities in previously held information. Specifically, while people from all strata may learn new information as a result of a mass media campaign, those with higher levels of education are likely to learn more than those with low levels of education, and the informational gap between the two groups will expand. The results of the analysis show that knowledge gaps do not always grow over the course of presidential campaigns and that some events, such as debates, may actually reduce the level of information inequality in the electorate.

Cultivation Theory

Cultivation theory (sometimes referred to as the cultivation hypothesis or cultivation analysis) was an approach developed by Professor George Gerbner, dean of the Annenberg School of Communications at the University of Pennsylvania. He began the 'Cultural Indicators' research project in the mid-1960s, to study whether and how watching television may influence viewers' ideas of what the everyday world is like. Cultivation research is in the 'effects' tradition. Cultivation theorists argue that television has long-term effects which are small, gradual, indirect but cumulative and significant.

They emphasize the effects of television viewing on the attitudes rather than the behaviour of viewers. Heavy watching of television is seen as 'cultivating' attitudes which are more consistent with the world of television programmes than with the everyday world. Watching television may tend to induce a general mindset about violence in the world, quite apart from any effects it might have in inducing violent behaviour. Cultivation theorists distinguish between 'first order' effects (general beliefs about the everyday world, such as about the prevalence of violence) and 'second order' effects (specific attitudes, such as to law and order or to personal safety).

Gerbner argues that the mass media cultivate attitudes and values which are already present in a culture: the media maintain and propagate these values amongst members of a culture, thus binding it together. He has argued that television tends to cultivate middle-of-the-road political perspectives. And Gross considered that 'television is a cultural arm of the established industrial order and as such serves primarily to maintain, stabilize and reinforce rather than to alter, threaten or weaken conventional beliefs and behaviours'. Such a function is conservative, but heavy viewers tend to regard themselves as 'moderate'.

Cultivation research looks at the mass media as a socializing agent and investigates whether television viewers come to believe the television version of reality the more they watch it. Gerbner and his colleagues contend that television drama has a small but significant influence on the attitudes, beliefs and judgements of viewers concerning the social world. The focus is on 'heavy viewers'. People who watch a lot of television are likely to be more influenced by the ways in which the world is framed by television programmes than are individuals who watch less, especially regarding topics of which the viewer has little first-hand experience. Light viewers may have more sources of information than heavy viewers. Judith van Evra argues that by virtue of inexperience, young viewers may depend on television for information more than other viewers do, although Hawkins and Pingree argue that some children may not experience a cultivation effect at all where they do not understand motives or consequences . It may be that lone viewers are more open to a cultivation effect than those who view with others.

Television is seen by Gerbner as dominating our 'symbolic environment'. As McQuail and Windahl note, cultivation theory presents television as 'not a window on or reflection of the world, but a world in itself'. Gerbner argued that the over-representation of violence on television constitutes a symbolic message about law and order rather than a simple cause of more aggressive behaviour by viewers (as Bandura argued). For instance, the action- adventure genre acts to reinforce a faith in law and order, the status quo and social justice.

Since 1967, Gerbner and his colleagues have been analysing sample weeks of prime-time and daytime television programming. Cultivation analysis usually involves the correlation of data from content analysis (identifying prevailing images on television) with survey data from audience research (to assess any influence of such images on the attitudes of viewers). Content analysis by cultivation theorists seeks to characterize 'the TV world'. Such analysis shows not only that the TV world is far more violent than the everyday world, but also, for instance, that television is dominated by males and over-represents the professions and those involved in law enforcement.

Audience research by cultivation theorists involves asking large-scale public opinion poll organizations to include in their national surveys questions regarding such issues as the amount of violence in everyday life. Answers are interpreted as reflecting either the world of television or that of everyday life. Respondents are asked such questions as: 'What percentage of all males who have jobs work in law enforcement or crime detection? Is it 1 percent or 10 percent?'. On American TV, about 12 percent of all male characters hold such jobs, and about 1 percent of males are employed in the USA in these jobs, so 10 percent would be the 'TV answer' and 1 percent would be the 'real-world answer'.

Answers are then related to the amount of television watched, other media habits and demographic data such as sex, age, income and education. The cultivation hypothesis involves predicting or expecting heavy television viewers to give more TV answers than light viewers. The responses of a large number of heavy viewers are compared with those of light viewers. A tendency of heavy viewers to choose TV answers is interpreted as evidence of a cultivation effect.

Cultivation theorists are best known for their study of television and viewers, and in particular for a focus on the topic of violence. However, some studies have also considered other mass media from this perspective, and have dealt with topics such as gender roles, age groups, ethnic groups and political attitudes. A study of American college students found that heavy soap opera viewers were more likely than light viewers to over-estimate the number of real-life married people who had affairs or who had been divorced and the number of women who had abortions.

The difference in the pattern of responses between light and heavy viewers (when other variables are controlled), is referred to as the 'cultivation differential', reflecting the extent to which an attitude seems to be shaped by watching television. Older people tend to be portrayed negatively on television and heavy viewers (especially younger ones) tend to hold more negative views about older people than lighter viewers. Most heavy viewers are unaware of any influence of television viewing on their attitudes and values.

Cultivation theorists argue that heavy viewing leads viewers (even among high educational/high income groups) to have more homogeneous or convergent opinions than light viewers. The cultivation effect of television viewing is one of 'levelling' or 'homogenizing' opinion. Gerbner and his associates argue that heavy viewers of violence on television come to believe that the incidence of violence in the everyday world is higher than do light viewers of similar backgrounds. They refer to this as a mainstreaming effect.

Misjudging the amount of violence in society is sometimes called the 'mean world syndrome'. Heavy viewers tend to believe that the world is a nastier place than do light viewers. Pingree and Hawkins studied 1,280 primary schoolchildren (2nd-11th grade) in Australia using viewing diaries and questionnaires. They found that heavy viewing led to a 'television-biased' view of Australia as a 'mean and violent' place. The children with the bleakest picture of Australia were those who most watched American crime adventure programmes. Oddly, they did not judge the USA to the same extent by these programmes.

Gerbner reported evidence for 'resonance' - a 'double dose' effect which may boost cultivation. This is held to occur when the viewer's everyday life experiences are congruent with those depicted in the television world. For instance, since on television women are most likely to be victims of crime, women heavy viewers are influenced by the usual heavy viewer mainstreaming effect but are also led to feel especially fearful for themselves as women. The cultivation effect is also argued to be strongest when the viewer's neighbourhood is similar to that shown on television. Crime on television is largely urban, so urban heavy viewers are subject to a double dose, and cultivation theorists argue that violent content 'resonates' more for them. The strongest effects of heavy viewing on attitudes to violence are likely to be amongst those in the high crime areas of cities.

5

Functions of Mass Media

The mass media can be traced to Gutenberg's printing presses, which copied vernacular Bibles in German and helped launch the Protestant Reformation. Today the media include not only books but radio, television, movies, periodicals such as comic books, newspapers and magazines, recording media such as videotapes, audiotapes and disks, and the increasingly popular CD-ROM. Regardless of the technology employed, all mass media share one major characteristic: they enable a relatively small number of individuals to communicate with a large, more or less impersonal, audience.

The overt functions of the mass media are quite obvious. Most of these media purport to entertain audiences with interesting stories or enticing aural or visual presentations. Other media, such as newspapers, many magazines and nonfiction books, provide information about the world. In addition are media of persuasion, such as advertising and, in totalitarian societies, political propaganda.

Perhaps the most significant covert role of the media is a kind of priestly function that helps the masses articulate their basic values and beliefs. This is especially true in a market system, where the economic goal of media is to maximize audiences for advertisers. In this context the media try to create messages that resonate with general consumer tastes and interests, as well as with fundamental values and beliefs. The major purpose of such media is not to alter audiences' perceptions as much as to tell audiences what they want to hear, to show them what they want to see and generally to confirm existing beliefs regardless of their validity or veracity.

This priestly function exists across the spectrum of informative, persuasive and entertaining media. News stories, for instance, implicitly take the viewpoint that evil results from the wicked actions of evil people, not from any human defect that would implicate the entire human race. Such a popular theology confirms the common precepts that audiences wish to believe, namely, that evil can be eliminated by removing evil people from society. Similarly, television commercials, billboards and magazine advertisements reinforce the public hope that various products and services can make anyone happy, beautiful or popular. Even the entertainment media join in this prophetic role by confirming a myth such as individualism through various narrative formulas. From a priestly perspective, the media accept the world the way it is and make it even more that way.

Media also function as prophets by purporting to bring truth to the people. We see this not just in news media (for example, newspaper columnists and TV-news anchors) but also in political talk-radio (thus saith the host), literature (novels that "reveal" aspects of life and the human condition) and cinema (the filmmaker's vision of the human condition). Media offer this type of prophetic word or image whenever they claim a new insight, privileged information or prescient knowledge.

Of course it is often difficult to determine the line between prophetic and priestly media without both critical discernment and a standard of truth external to the media. A popular political talk-show host and an established highbrow novelist may seem to have little in common when in fact each one panders his or her prophetic insights to a particular audience predisposed to such beliefs.

In many parts of the world, the mass media have a growing cultural influence over all areas of life. Most importantly they compete for authority with local nurturing institutions, including the family, schools and churches. This tension creates waves of antagonisms between media elites and the leaders of local groups who feel that their ways of life are threatened by the media. Many of the battles over sex, violence and profanity in the media, for example, are rooted in conflicting moral standards represented by Hollywood (or the Western world) on the one hand and particular religious, ethnic or nationalistic identities on the other.

While some groups merely criticize the media, others take the more positive approach of establishing their own, alternative media. The trend toward mass media is always challenged by this countervailing force of media that serve distinct cultural, even religious, groups. Christians, for example, have their own publishing houses, periodicals, radio and television stations and networks, and recording industry. Ironically, evangelicals often view these specialized media as evangelism when, in fact, distinctly Christian media rarely appeal to the broader culture.

Newer electronic media also promise to give religious groups an opportunity to organize in opposition to mainstream media. Fax machines, satellites and especially electronic mail (computer-to-computer communication) are important challenges to traditional broadcasting and publishing. It remains to be seen, however, whether new media will eventually become merely a part of the existing media empires, commercial or ideological.

MASS MEDIA AS FOURTH ESTATE

The mass media are often attacked by left-wing critics: from within the broadly Marxist vein of critical theory they are criticized for reproducing the dominant bourgeois culture; from within the 'political economy' vein of research, they are attacked for representing the interests of those who own them.

However, from the perspective of those researchers who see the media as situated within the model of a pluralist liberal democracy, the mass media are often seen as fulfilling the vitally important role of *fourth estate*, the guardians of democracy, defenders of the public interest.

The term fourth estate is frequently attributed to the nineteenth century historian Carlyle, though he himself seems to have attributed it to Edmund Burke:

> Burke said there were Three Estates in Parliament; but, in the Reporters' Gallery yonder, there sat a Fourth Estate more important than they all. It is not a figure of speech, or a witty saying; it is a literal fact, ... Printing, which comes necessarily out of Writing, I say often, is equivalent to Democracy: invent Writing, Democracy is inevitable. ..... Whoever can speak, speaking now to the whole nation, becomes a power, a branch of government, with inalienable weight in law-making, in all acts of authority. It matters not what rank he has, what revenues or garnitures: the requisite thing is that he have a tongue which others will listen to; this and nothing more is requisite.

Carlyle here was describing the newly found power of the man of letters, and, by extension, the newspaper reporter. In his account, it seems that the press are a new fourth estate added to the three existing estates (as they were conceived of at the time) running the country: priesthood, aristocracy and commons. Other modern commentators seem to interpret the term fourth estate as meaning the fourth 'power' which checks and counterbalances the three state 'powers' of executive, legislature and judiciary.

In recent years increasing attention has been paid by media theorists to the notion of the public sphere as developed by German philosopher Jürgen Habermas. Habermas, implacable opponent of postmodernist theorizing, argues that in eighteenth century England there was the emergence of a 'public sphere ... which mediates between society and state', in which 'the public organises itself as the bearer of public opinion'.

Simultaneously with the growth of urban culture, where there was the development of a new arena of public life (theatres, museums, opera houses, coffee houses, etc.), there was also the growth of a new infrastructure for social communication (the press, publishing houses, libraries), together with increased literacy and better transportation. These communication webs allowed discussion of matters which branched out from relatively small groups into affairs of the state and of politics. According to Habermas, these led to increased social intercourse.

Rather differently from Carlyle, Habermas emphasizes that the public sphere *was* class-linked and therefore accessible only to members of the bourgeoisie. As Habermas sees it, any member of the bourgeoisie who had access to the technology was able to join in popular cultural debate based on a firm faith in the value of reasoned discussion. As Mark Poster succinctly summarizes the idea,

> Although the public sphere never included everyone, and by itself did not determine the outcome of all parliamentary actions, it contributed to the spirit of dissent found in a healthy representative democracy.

In fact perhaps the most evocative description of that kind of public sphere is to be found in Neil Postman's description of eighteenth century America, a society in which literacy was vastly more widespread and democratized than in the Britain of the time. Postman is also concerned to show how print literacy in itself encourages rational and ordered thinking, participation in contemporary debate and the ability to understand and follow detailed and complex argument.

Incidentally, the similarity of Habermas's claimed development of a public sphere to the current development of the Internet is striking and probably accounts in part for the renewed interest in his idea, some thirty odd years after it was first aired. It has also no doubt come to be seen as an increasingly important question as increasing globalization undermines the power of the nation-state and the legitimacy of national democracies. As our traditional forms of representative, democratic politics apparently decline in relevance, as participation in such politics declines and citizens turn towards identity-based 'single issues', how can we develop a meaningful concept of the public sphere?

Habermas identified a variety of liberal-bourgeois rights which guaranteed the operation of the various spheres and their institutions:

> A set of basic rights concerned the sphere of the public engaged in rational-critical debate (freedom of opinion and speech, freedom of press, freedom of assembly and association etc.) and the political function of private people in this public sphere (rights of petition, equality of vote etc.). A second set of basic rights concerned the individual's status as a free human being, grounded in the intimate sphere of the patriarchal conjugal family (personal freedom, inviolability of the home etc.). The third set of basic rights concerned the transactions of the private owners of property in the sphere of civil society (equality before the law, protection of private property etc.). The basic rights guaranteed: the *spheres* of the public realm and of the private (with the intimate sphere at its core); the *institutions* and *instruments* of the public sphere, on the one hand (press, parties), and the foundation of private autonomy (family and property), on the other; finally, the *functions* of the private people, both their political ones as citizens and their economic ones as owners of commodities (and, as 'human beings', those of individual communication, e.g. through inviolability of letters).

This 'bourgeois public sphere' is seen by Habermas, then, as an area of informed, public and reasoned debate, to which the emergence of an independent, market-based press was crucial. It was open to a large number of people, within it various arguments and views were subjected to rational discussion and government policies were systematically submitted to its critical scrutiny.

However, according to Habermas, after the first half of the nineteenth century the situation changed, as the public sphere became dominated by a strong, expanded state and a press which represented organized economic interests. The media, from having been part of the public sphere of reasoned discussion, became part of the process of 're-feudalization' of the public sphere as state, industrial conglomerates and the media undergo a process of fusion. The media became the manipulators of public opinion, conditioning the public into the rôle of passive onlookers and consumers. Similarly to Habermas, Elliott argues that in 1980s Britain technological and economic developments were promoting a continuation of the shift away from involving people in societies as political citizens of nation states towards involving them as consumption units in a corporate world.

The 'fourth estate', 'guardians of the public sphere' become increasingly converted into industries, wholly oriented towards the profit motive, just another business held by some conglomerate. For Habermas the decline of the public sphere is linked to the triumph of instrumental rationality which he later discusses at length in his *Theory of Communicative Action* Habermas pleads for the revivification of the 'lifeworld' which operates according to principles of communicative rationality, but which has been 'uncoupled' from 'system' which operates according to principles of money and power, reward and punishment. The instrumental rationality of the system invades or 'colonizes' the lifeworld and thereby erodes the public sphere.

McGuigan takes as an example the Thatcherisation of Independent Television in the UK, after which casualisation, poor pay and overwork all grew apace. Colin Sparks has likened the resultant labour market to a peasant economy: '[Independents] are the industrial equivalent of small peasants who work themselves and their families to death in order to hold onto the family plot after the realities of the market place have dictated that it would be rational to sell up to a large capitalist farmer and move to the city to find work.' Is this, then, the 'refeudalization of the public sphere' at the point of production? The robber barons themselves now raid on a much grander scale than in medieval times, organizing neo-feudal relations of production and consumption in the burgeoning information industries across the globe.

The output of the robber barons' media no longer, in Habermas's view, can be seen as contributing to rational discourse in the public sphere. Rather it serves merely to entertain and turn the potential participants in the public sphere into mere passive consumers. Despite the radically different views held by Habermas and Baudrillard, the picture Habermas paints is not all that different in essence from Baudrillard's claim in *In the Shadow of Silent Majorities* that people simply don't care about 'the issues'. Baudrillard's *silent passivities* would equate, in Habermas's terms to a failure to take part in rational-critical debate.

Habermas's *re-feudalization* is Baudrillard's *simulation* of debate by TV politicians. It would seem fairly clear that Habermas's portrayal of the re-feudalization of the public sphere is influenced by Adorno's and Horkheimer's portrayal of the operation and effects of the 'culture industries' and equally clear that he would not take quite the same view today. Apart from the thesis of the public sphere overstating and idealizing the free debate of the eighteenth century, it also overstates the 'dumbing-down' thesis of modern media effects, assuming that the content of certain media products necessarily engenders passivity and false consciousness. Certainly, modern politicians attempt to manage the media agenda, certainly they rely on their spin doctors to present the right image, but in the eighteenth century they bribed voters and got them drunk on election day. The increasing mediazation of modern culture has been accompanied by increasing democratization, so media exposure cuts both ways.

Mass media as Watchdog

It probably doesn't matter a great deal what Carlyle originally meant; similarly, it's probably of no great importance that Habermas has been criticized for idealizing the supposed period of informed public debate. What is important is that both writers paint a powerful picture of the media participating in the maintenance of the public sphere as a kind of neutral zone in which people organize and debate collectively and rationally for the benefit of the common good and contributing to the development of democratic debate. Thus, the term 'fourth estate' is used today to refer to the mass media as a powerful watchdog in liberal democracy, revealing abuses of state authority and defending the democratic rights of citizens.

Media Independence

Not surprisingly, since this view of the media's fourth estate function is rooted within the pluralist liberal democracy model, it is commonly accompanied by an assumption that the media, in order to act as fourth estate, must be independent of the state. In other words, the watchdog function can only be fulfilled by a free market organization of the media. It is assumed that, if the watchdog is subject to state regulation, then it will become the state's poodle.

This argument has been used to legitimate the increasing deregulation of American and British broadcasting over the last decade or so. The regulation of broadcasting was originally tolerated because the relatively limited number of frequencies available meant that franchises had necessarily to be limited. Therefore, since some had to be excluded from obtaining a franchise (a restriction which did not apply to anyone wishing to launch a press title), there was a requirement in both countries of some measure of public service broadcasting, which to an extent would cater for the interests of those excluded from a franchise. However, the development of cable and satellite TV has meant that in the USA people can choose from more TV stations than newspapers and in Great Britain from at least as many. The deregulation of broadcasting, from this point of view, therefore becomes a legitimate goal, since, it can be argued, that will ensure broadcasting's independence of the state.

Whilst in Britain the deregulation of the media has continued apace, a move justified in part by the desirability of reducing the interference of the 'nanny-state', this has not been accompanied by any significant liberalization of the Official Secrets Act . Despite New Labour's professed intentions of introducing a Freedom of Information Act, nothing has yet been passed into law and the proposals so far made for such an Act could hardly be recognized as promoting freedom of information. At present it remains unclear what will be the effect of the European Convention on Human Rights, now part of UK law. Article 10 of the Convention prescribes a basic right to freedom of expression, which should be restricted only for pressing reasons of the public interest.

During the early months of 1998, US media organizations have repeatedly had to issue apologies for misreporting. *The New Republic* discovered that certain articles by one of its most favoured young reporters were fabrications; the *Boston Globe*'s Patricia Smith resigned after admitting to inventing characters in four 1998 columns; *Time* magazine at the time of writing is investigating what it suspects is untrue reporting in in its columns and on *CNN* regarding claims of US troops using nerve gas against other US troops in South-East Asia. A *New York Times* editor ascribed this current surge in misreporting to 'a massively increased sensitivity to all things financial'.

This is in part due to the operation of the global free market as we see it operating in other spheres too: mergers into huge corporations, with the usual attendant reductions in staff and staff training in order to maximize shareholders' dividends, shareholders who are to a great extent composed of retirement funds and insurance companies who will soon shift their stock elsewhere if they can get a higher return. In part it is probably also due to the increased competition arising from the use of new technologies. Photos are transmitted digitally, stories are e-mailed from across the globe, and perhaps more importantly scoops are announced on Web sites by freelancers running their own fairly small and cheap set-ups; 'freebooters' might be a more accurate term as some of them don't seem overly scrupulous about checking their facts. In such circumstances, the conventional media can be easily scooped by a small Web organization.

As a signal of the shift from hard to soft news, Neil Hickey of the Columbia Journalism Review examined the cover stories of *Time* and *Newsweek* in 1987 and 1997. In 1987, *Time* had eleven covers relating to foreign news; in 1997, only one. Domestic hard news covers reduced from twelve to nine. In other words, the overall total for straight news dropped from around 45% in 1987 to 20% in 1997. Obsession with ratings, says Hickey, is 'at an all-time high' in TV newsrooms, where, until recently, ratings were largely an irrelevance, the emphasis being on news coverage. The broadcasters and the press editors respond to criticism by saying that the US public are currently not concerned with hard news as the economy is prospering and are not concerned with foreign news since the collapse of the USSR. In giving the public soft news, the media are merely giving the public what they want. To some that may sound like the way a democracy should function, but, in response to this argument Hickey quotes the former President of NBC News, Reuven Frank:

> This business of giving people what they want is a dope-pusher's argument. News is something people don't know they're interested in until they hear about it. The job of a journalist is to take what's important and make it interesting.

Another factor which needs to be borne in mind is the increasing concentration of media ownership and the merger of media organizations with non-media corporations. It could be argued that, with the declining rôle of national state governments and the increasing power of transnational corporations, the media watchdog should pay more attention to abuses by global capitalist institutions than by the state. And here, of course, is the rub.

The supporters of the free, deregulated media market argue vociferously that media institutions must be independent of the state otherwise they will be in some way beholden to it. The argument runs, for example, that such media will think twice before criticizing the government of the day for fear of losing subsidies or of provoking restrictive legislation. So newspaper editors in Britain have campaigned against the introduction of any kind of right to privacy. Pressure for such legislation has mounted as the press have become increasingly intrusive in their coverage of royalty, celebrities and MPs. The British press point to the example of France, where there is an established right to privacy and where, as a result - or so they claim - the press is the government's lapdog.

Similarly, Rupert Murdoch, owner of News Corp., for instance, claimed that the price paid by British broadcasters for their privileges was their freedom. From this argument, though, it surely follows logically that those media which are owned by major corporations must be beholden to those corporations, a corollary which Mr Murdoch chooses to overlook.

When Carlyle advanced his notion of the fourth estate, he said that for anyone to become 'a power, a branch of government' in the nation 'the requisite thing is that he have a tongue which others will listen to; this and nothing more is requisite'. Carlyle is speaking here of the Habermasian public sphere in which a range of relatively small partisan presses present their views, which are taken up in discussion, fed back into, and commented on in, those presses in open and rational debate.

As Habermas sees it, early capitalism was compelled to resist the s'ate, hence the drive for a free press, open discussion of state affairs and the demand for political reform and greater representation. However, as capitalism gathered impetus, it moved from calls for reform of the state to the take-over of the state. Once the capitalist state was in being with the corporate financing of lobbyists and government think tanks, MPs' directorships, the injection of business funds into parties' election campaigns and so on, the media's rôle underwent a significant change, in Habermas's view: where they had once been providers of information and argument to the neutral public sphere, they became manufacturers and manipulators of public opinion. The public sphere became a fake.

Thirty years after Habermas first sketched his gloomy vision of the collapse of the public sphere, the media have progressed ever further towards concentration of ownership, ever further towards monopoly capitalism. Murdoch's News Corp, for example owns around 60% of metropolitan daily circulation in Australia, Fox TV,

Twentieth Century Fox, a controlling interest in BSkyB, Star TV, Times Newspapers, The Sun newspaper as well as magazine and book publishers including Harper Collins and Triangle. The enormous wealth and global reach of such media organizations is unprecedented, with the result that the free play of market forces hardly allows a level playing field.

Does it necessarily follow that, because ownership is concentrated, because media conglomerates and the state share common interests, the media are powerful shapers of public opinion? It is a widely held view that that does follow - for example after the 1992 General Election, won by the Conservatives after confident predictions of a Labour victory, the Sun newspaper proclaimed triumphantly in a banner headline: 'It's the Sun wot won it!'; Lord McAlpine, Conservative Party treasurer, thanked the Conservative press for securing the victory; Neil Kinnock, the Labour leader, blamed the Conservative press for Labour's defeat. There is plenty of evidence from the reception studies of the 'new audience research', though, that there is no such simple linkage between the views expressed by the media and people's political choices. Reception studies show that readers do readily develop oppositional readings of media texts.

Mass Media Simulate Political Transparency

Without mass media, openness and accountability are impossible in contemporary democracies. Nevertheless, mass media can hinder political transparency as well as help it. Politicians and political operatives can simulate the political virtues of transparency through rhetorical and media manipulation. Political life begins to conform increasingly to the image of politics portrayed on television. Through a quasi-Darwinian process, media events, scandals, and other forms of politics-as-entertainment eventually dominate and weed out other forms of political information and public discussion, transforming the very meaning of public discourse. In this way the goals of political transparency can be defeated by what appear to be its central mechanisms: proliferating information, holding political officials accountable for their actions, and uncovering secrets.

This section concerns the mass media's contributions to the political values of openness and democratic accountability that go by the name of 'transparency.' In fact, the metaphor of transparency encompasses three separate political virtues, which often work together but are analytically distinct. The first kind of transparency is informational transparency: knowledge about government actors and decisions and access to government information. Informational transparency can be furthered by requiring public statements of the reasons for government action, or requiring disclosure of information the government has collected. A second type of transparency is participatory transparency: the ability to participate in political decisions either through fair representation or direct participation. A third kind of transparency is accountability transparency: the ability to hold government officials accountable – either to the legal system or to public opinion – when they violate the law or when they act in ways that adversely affect people's interests.

In theory, at least, mass media can make the political system more 'transparent' in all three respects: mass media can help people understand the operations of government, participate in political decisions, and hold government officials accountable. In practice, however, its effects are often quite different. In the age of mass media, democratic governments and politicians may find it useful to simulate the political virtues of transparency through rhetorical and media manipulation. This simulated transparency does not serve the underlying political values that motivate the metaphor of transparency. Instead, it is a transparency that obscures and obfuscates, that frustrates accountability and hides important information in a mass of manufactured political realities. It is a form of transparency that is not transparent at all.

Today political transparency is virtually impossible without some form of mass media coverage. However, mass media can frustrate the values of political transparency even while appearing to serve those values. When politicians and political operatives attempt to simulate transparency and appropriate the rhetoric of openness and accountability, the mass media does not always counteract the simulation. Indeed, it may actually tend to proliferate it.

People often oppose transparency to secrecy. However, governments and politicians can manipulate the presentation and revelation of information to achieve the same basic goals as a policy of secrecy and obfuscation. There are two basic strategies: divert audience attention, and supplement politics with new realities that crowd out and eventually displace other political realties and political issues. In this way political transparency can be defeated by what appear to be its own mechanisms: proliferating information, holding political officials accountable, and uncovering things that are secret. The very metaphor of transparency suggests a medium through which we view things. We want the medium to be transparent to vision so that we can accurately view what is on the other side. This metaphor assumes:

(1) That the medium is conceptually separate from the object on the other side; and

(2) That the process of seeing through the medium does not substantially alter the nature of the object viewed.

Both of these assumptions turn out to be false when the medium is television and the object to be viewed is governance. The medium is not conceptually distinct from the operations of governance because governance occurs through using the medium. Moreover, seeing things through the medium of television substantially alters the object being viewed. Indeed, television creates its own political reality: a televised politics and a public sphere of discourse organised around media coverage of politics. This sphere of discourse is self-reflexive and self-reproducing – television coverage of politics is part of politics, and hence media discourse about politics continually supplements and alters the politics that it purports to portray.

How do mass media simulate and subvert political transparency? The basic idea is simple. Sometimes the most effective strategy for hiding something may be to leave it out in the open, and merely alter the context in which people view it. Instead of hiding facts, one should instead seek to change background realities. Large law firms in the United States have long understood this point. When faced with requests for discovery in civil cases, they understand that simply stonewalling to avoid the disclosure of sensitive information is not always the most effective strategy. Instead they can adopt a dual strategy of aggressive overcompliance coupled with strategic manoeuvre. They flood the other side with so much information and so many documents – most of them extraneous – that the other side lacks the time or ability to find the relevant information. At the same time, the law firm can raise continual technical objections to the progress of discovery, without ever ultimately withholding anything.

These tactics are most useful against a weaker, smaller opponent with less information processing and filtering resources. They are designed to demoralise the other side, raise the costs of litigation, and divert time and energy from the most important substantive questions in the lawsuit. In this way one can use the discovery process –

which is, after all, designed to achieve a certain kind of informational transparency – to undermine the values of transparency. One can use the form of transparency to achieve substantial obscurity.

This example demonstrates the two basic strategies for simulating transparency: diversion of attention and supplementation of reality. The goal is to consume the opponent's time and attention. Equally important, one tries to shift the ground of battle to issues of information management and technical questions of procedure. In short, one creates a new practical legal reality for the opponent. This new reality competes with and displaces the substantive issues that originally motivated the lawsuit. In other words, the skilfully played discovery battle creates new objects of contention: it produces ever new things to be concerned about, to become angry about, and to fight about.

In the public arena, simulation of transparency also uses diversion and supplementation. But although the public is trying to obtain information, it is not in the same position as a litigant. Politicians and the mass media do not necessarily regard the public as an adversary. Rather politicians seek to shape and benefit from public opinion, and mass media seek to entertain the public and maintain public attention and influence. Nevertheless, in achieving these ends politicians and the media, both collectively and agonistically, divert audience attention and supplement politics with new political realities.

Role of Television

Many different kinds of mass media can simulate transparency. But the dominant medium of political communication in our age – and hence the dominant medium of political transparency – is television. To understand how television simulates transparency, we must understand how television shapes what we see through it. When we use television to understand politics, we see things in the way that television allows them to be seen. At the same time, television creates new forms of political reality that exist because they are seen on television.

Television tends to emphasise entertainment value. It subjects culture to a Darwinian process: The less entertaining is weeded out, the more entertaining survives to be broadcast. Hence coverage of public events, politics, and even law must eventually conform to the requirements of 'good television,' that is, the kind of television that grabs and keeps viewers' attention by absorbing and entertaining them. Television encourages coverage that focuses on the personal celebrity of participants and on the sporting elements of political conflict. Over time, television coverage of politics tends to focus less on substantive policy issues than on the techniques of securing political advantage and political viability. The question of 'who's winning' and how are they achieving this victory tends to dominate television coverage. In one sense stories about backstage political manoeuvring and spin control offer a kind of transparency, because they purport to give viewers an 'inside' account of the strategic considerations of politicians and public officials. But in another sense they divert attention from substantive policy debates. Given the limited time available for broadcast and the limited attention of audiences, 'inside' stories about strategy and jockeying for political advantage tend to crowd out stories about substantive policy questions.

Moreover, because politicians understand how important mass media have become to retaining power and influencing citizens, television helps create a new reality populated by spin doctors, pollsters, pundits and media consultants. Thus eventually political life begins to conform more closely to the image of politics that television portrays it to be. Television portrays a world of image manipulation and spin control largely devoid of substantive debate or reasoned analysis. Because television is so central to successful mass politics, it eventually helps produce the very elements that it portrays. We might call this a self-fulfilling representation.

Television coverage of law has analogous effects. Television converts law into a form of entertainment suitable for consumption by lay audiences. Television has created a world of law-related shows and legal commentators whose basic goal is to describe law in ways that are comprehensible to television audiences and that can hold their attention. This means, among other things, that law must become entertaining. Certain features of law – the thrust and parry of contention in lawsuits and criminal trials – seem tailor made for television coverage. But the image of law that television portrays reshapes the adversary system in television's image.

Law-as-entertainment seems to bring the legal system closer to the public, but it actually substitutes a transformed product – televised law. Public imagination about law used to be nourished by television dramas and made-for-TV movies; now it is increasingly shaped by television coverage of legal events themselves which are served up as popular entertainment and displayed through the lens of television commentary.

In a very short time the Internet has become an important medium of political communication that rivals television. The Internet is not yet televisual; it employs mostly text and still pictures. Even so, the Internet has shaped and enhanced the effects of television in three ways. First, the Internet has helped to shorten the news cycle of reporting, in part because stories can be constantly updated on the Internet with relative ease. A shorter news cycle tends to promote more continuous television coverage of news events, especially on cable networks.

Second, because the Internet makes mass distribution of information relatively inexpensive, it helps proliferate new kinds of information from new sources – including gossip and second-hand reports – that television can pick up and disseminate, assuming that the information passes muster under existing standards of television journalism. Third, for similar reasons, the Internet makes possible new journalistic sources that compete with television coverage, and new journalistic practices that may occasionally affect the form and content of television coverage and the standards of television journalists. Hence, the Internet can help exacerbate television's tendency to emphasise celebrity, inside strategy and gossip, and television's conversion of law and politics into forms of entertainment, even though the Internet is not yet a fully televisual medium.

Media Events

Media events are familiar methods of manipulating political transparency. Politicians stage events specifically designed to be covered by the mass media. Media events show politicians engaged in the business of governing or carefully deliberating over public policy issues. Another class of media event shows the politician with his or her family, participating in casual activities, or in a seemingly unguarded and intimate moment.

Media events that involve displays of governance are designed to look governmental, and media events involving displays of personal affect are designed to look spontaneous. American politics has employed media events for many years. The Reagan Administration developed them to a high art form. Almost all public presidential appearances now consist in some form of media event, merging the act of governance with media display. The Clinton Administration has used media events to great advantage: As President Clinton lost the ability to push large scale reforms through a recalcitrant Congress, he increasingly took to governing through small scale initiatives like encouraging the adoption of school uniforms. These initiatives were announced and touted in a series of media events designed to make his presidency appear active, robust, and engaged with popular sentiments and concerns.

Media events perform a *jujitsu* move on the political values of transparency. The goal of political transparency is to help people watch over the operations of government and the behaviour of government officials. The point of the media event is to encourage watching. The media event is a form of political exhibitionism that simulates effective governance and personal candour.

By demanding our attention, and the attention of the news media, media events appear to offer us substantive information although what they actually offer is largely political image and showmanship. Moreover, by commanding media attention, media events trade on a fundamental difficulty facing all forms of political transparency. This is the problem of audience scarcity.

Most individuals have only limited time and attention to devote to public issues. Political values of transparency do not demand that citizens spend all of their time on public subjects. Rather, they make information available to individuals so that they can use it if they so choose. But when there is too much information, filtering necessarily occurs. This filtering occurs both in terms of what media decide to cover and what individuals decide to watch. Media companies must pick and choose among hundreds of possible subjects to discuss. Individuals must choose among thousands of hours of potential coverage of public events.

The need for filtering enhances the power of media events. By flooding the media with ready made press releases and staged pageants that function as 'good television,' politicians provide media with easily edited programming that can be strung together in televised sequences. Providing media with 'good television' allows politicians to capture more and more of the media's coverage. This diverts media attention from information that might actually be more useful to the political goals of participation, information, and accountability.

Moreover, media events do not simply add new information to the mix; they also drive out other forms of coverage through a sort of Gresham's law of mass media. The media event is deliberately designed to be a watchable, ready-made form of political entertainment, one that can be easily chopped up and edited for news broadcasts. It is relatively cheap to cover, and easy to broadcast. News organisations quickly learn that it takes less effort to accept what is given them by politicians than to develop entertaining news programming on their own.

For these reasons media events can affect the behaviour of news organisations that are fully aware of their simulated character. Well-planned media events can displace other forms of reporting that take greater time and effort to produce. By thrusting entertainment in our face, politicians effectively keep us from watching other things. And because politicians, and especially presidents, increasingly govern through media events, news organisations feel an obligation to cover them. Media events, in short, both divert political attention and supplement political reality.

Mass Media in Public and Private Life

Many people have noted and decried the mass media's increasing intrusion into the private lives of public figures. Although coverage of entertainers' and sports figures' private lives has been common for many years, the phenomenon has clearly invaded political life as well. The Clinton scandals have made possible discussion of private sexual conduct in the mainstream press that would have been unthinkable only a few years before.

Media coverage of the private lives of public figures is actually a form of informational transparency, although not necessarily one that serves democratic values. Increasingly the mass media have endeavoured to make the private lives of public figures transparent to the ordinary viewer. For many people this evolution of journalistic standards is a travesty, because it diverts attention from 'public' issues. But as noted before, increasing intrusion into private lives does not merely divert attention – it also helps create and supplement public discourse; it fosters new political realities that cannot easily be avoided, as politicians ranging from Gary Hart to Bill Clinton have discovered to their chagrin. Repeated focus on the 'private' eventually alters the boundaries between public and private; it changes the nature of what is appropriately withheld from public scrutiny.

Revelations of the previously 'private' also alter the meaning of 'public discourse' or 'public issues.' The very pervasiveness and availability of information (or rumours) about the private lives of public officials reinforces the idea that such private behaviour is not wholly private – that it raises public issues about which the public should be concerned. In the 1992 and 1996 presidential campaigns Clinton's opponents used the term 'character issue' to show the connection between things formerly thought private and public concerns.

The character issue was not an artificial creation of Clinton's Republican opponents. It was fostered by repeated media investigations into the private lives of many different public officials before Clinton, and it was encouraged by the changes in public discourse brought about by these investigations. Journalists, in turn, have adapted the rhetoric of political transparency to defend their emerging investigative practices, to rationalise greater sexual frankness in reporting of news stories, and to justify their sense of greater entitlement to investigate and report on the private lives of public officials, including their infidelities, their sexual orientations, and their sexual habits.

Many journalists defend their evolving practices using language that sounds very much like a defence of political transparency: The public, they argue, has a right to know. Moreover, although some revelations may ultimately prove immaterial to political issues, journalists should place all potentially relevant information before the public and let the public choose whether it is relevant to democratic decision making. This rhetoric has three effects.

First, it equates public knowledge about (for example) the President's sexual habits with public knowledge about the details of foreign or domestic policy, and with information that government collects on private citizens through surveillance.

Second, by making these new forms of knowledge part of democratic decision-making, journalists change the contours of public discourse and the definition of a 'public issue.' Journalists do not simply respect the existing boundaries of the public and the private but actively reshape them. Merely by talking about sexual scandal and encouraging others to do so, journalists make these topics part of public discourse and public comment.

Third, by adding formerly excised information about sexual conduct to public discourse, journalists inevitably create competition for public attention between stories about politicians' private lives and stories about other aspects of public concern, for example, the details of public policy debates. In this competition, stories about sexual and personal matters are likely to grab a greater share of attention. By adding sexual scandal to the mix of competing stories, journalists change the odds that other forms of information will survive the inevitable filtering that occurs when information is too plentiful. It is somewhat like introducing a particularly virulent weed into a flower garden: one should not be surprised if the weed monopolises increasing amounts of space while less hardy plants are choked off.

This effect occurs even if the public does not think that 'private' or sexual matters are appropriate to judging the performance of public officials. For what draws audience attention is not what the public regards as relevant to public policy but what it regards as entertaining. For example, polls have repeatedly suggested that most Americans do not think President Clinton's alleged peccadillos undermine their confidence in his performance as president, although they have undermined their respect for him.

Nevertheless, the details of the Lewinsky scandal formed continuous fodder for talk shows, and for months consumed a considerable portion of nightly news broadcasts. Reports about scandal grab attention even if the scandal itself is considered irrelevant to public policy by the very public that watches the reports. As a result, the purported expansion of information in the name of 'the public's right to know' is effectively a contraction of public discourse, because audience time is limited. Through a Darwinian mechanism, information about sexual scandal proliferates and drives out information that constitutes or could potentially constitute other elements of public discourse.

The very question of what is appropriately a 'public issue' or an 'appropriate' story to broadcast is not based on a fixed set of standards. Rather, it is the product of the joint activities of all who call themselves journalists, and depends on their existing professional standards and their expectations about likely public reaction to their reports. Because each journalist has the potential ability to alter the mix of stories competing in the public sphere, journalists as a whole face a collective action problem in maintaining the boundaries of what is public and what is private. If one journalist changes the contours of the public through a series of revelations, other journalists may feel compelled to follow along. Journalists may feel duty bound to report whatever is in fact in the public sphere of discussion. Once one journalist has broken a story, it has been inserted into the public arena, thus lessening the sense of responsibility felt by other journalists.

Moreover, once a story has been inserted into public discussion, the incentives of media actors follow a familiar logic: Because journalists believe that certain kinds of stories are more likely to gain valuable and limited audience attention than others, they must respond when other journalists produce stories likely to garner the lion's share of attention because of their salacious or dramatic elements. The result is a self-amplifying focus or a 'feeding frenzy' around certain topics.

It is important to recognise that this effect can occur even though all journalists do not share the same standards of what is newsworthy. It can occur even though mainstream or high prestige journalists usually demand more corroboration or more reliable sources than other journalists before they will publish a story. For example, journalists in traditional metropolitan dailies take great pains to distinguish their standards and practices from those of Matt Drudge's Drudge Report. Drudge's Internet-based column regularly acts as a foil to the journalistic standards of the mainstream media. However, once a journalist like Drudge publishes a story, this sends a few journalists scurrying to confirm it. If they cannot confirm it according to their higher standards, the story does not spread to more mainstream outlets. However, once there is confirming evidence – as judged by the standards of a given group of professional journalists – there is pressure on those journalists to repeat the substance of the story. Eventually this creates a sort of cascade effect. This cascade occurs even if there are different groups of journalists with different standards of verification. And once a story breaks through a certain level of 'mainstream' journalistic judgement, it is very difficult to stop the story.

Fourth, by arguing that the public has a right to know about 'private' issues, journalists can present themselves as more devoted to transparency than journalists of the past. While journalists previously would have killed stories about private sexual behaviour, contemporary journalists can claim that they are offering a freer, more open form of public debate in which they no longer play the role of paternalistic gatekeepers. Some journalists can even convince themselves that they are empowering the public through these revelations. But instead of empowering their audiences or increasing information, journalists may in fact simply be altering the mix of stories presented to the public; the practical effect may be a contraction of the scope of public discourse.

However, we should not lay blame for these changes entirely at the feet of journalists and media executives. In fact, politicians themselves have contributed to the gradual change in the contours of public discussion. Politicians, like other public figures, have discovered over time that in a world shaped by television, it is increasingly important to communicate not only information but also ethos. Public figures hope to persuade and possibly manipulate their audiences by presenting themselves as likeable or down-to-earth characters that a television audience can relate to. Using television to humanise public figures is related to the rise of media events as a form of governance.

By displaying their personalities for consumption by television audiences, public figures simulate yet another form of transparency – the transparency of ethos. The television audience gains access to what the public figure is 'really' like 'up close and personal.' Celebrities and public figures who appear regularly appear on television try to garner high popularity ratings by appearing close to their viewers. In this respect television differs somewhat from motion pictures; movie actors may deliberately attempt to establish aloofness or distance from their fans. Fans of television actors, on the other hand, often think themselves closer to the actors as people.

Politicians have learned that the appearance of intimacy or the production of an attractive ethos on television is very helpful to political success. As a result, many public figures have attempted to project as far as possible a personable, warm, or approachable image appropriate for television. Public figures who appear distant, cold, or uncaring on television generally succeed in spite of their appearance.

In order to simulate a transparency of ethos, politicians and public figures have been collapsing the distance between the public figure and his or her private persona for some time. They have attempted to connect with viewers and voters by emphasising their emotional availability, friendliness, and closeness to voters in ways dictated by the medium of television. Successful politicians have always run on character issues and emphasised their own good character. But television culture gradually changes the sort of character the successful politician must portray.

To succeed as a television personality, politicians have tended to emphasise elements of their persona that might otherwise be thought 'private;' they have shown more and more of their (seemingly) 'private' sides to the public. They show themselves to be 'family people.' They engage in confessional displays, revealing private features of their past, their family's past, or their family's current difficulties. They provide seemingly unguarded moments of revelation and deep connection to the voters. They emote on cue in public. To a large extent this presentation of the private side of a politician's life is a fabrication – it is the work of publicity agents and campaign staffs. Nevertheless, politicians persist in it because it works well in terms of the dominant medium of political communication – television.

But this simulated transparency comes at a cost. Simulating a transparent ethos for television necessarily reconfigures the boundaries between publicity and privacy. The more politicians attempt to use television as a means of establishing closeness to their constituents, the more they erase the boundaries between the public official and what they promote as his or her private persona. The exhibition of a private persona for public consumption invites the public to expect that elements of the private appropriately merge with a politician's public persona and hence are appropriate subjects of public discussion. Politicians have manipulated television imagery for so long that they have helped to create the very erasure of public and private persona that now haunts them. They have been willing accomplices in the creation of a new political culture that sees private aspects of a person's life as politically relevant, that collapses older boundaries between public and private.

6

Mass Media and Culture

We all inhabit particular situations and things like our surroundings, family, friends; school, work, neighbourhood and so on shape our individual identities. In media-speak we refer to this aspect of our cultural identity as our situated culture. In other words, the small-scale communications and interactions we have on a day-to-day basis with the place we live in and the people around us. This kind of culture is primarily an oral one - it is passed on and formed largely by intimate word-of-mouth communication.

Since the mid 19th century, we have come to live not only in a situated culture, but in a culture of mediation. The press, film and cinema, television and radio and more recently, the Internet, have developed to supply larger scale means of public communication. So now our situated culture exists within a much wider mediated world. The introduction of the term 'global village' in the 1960's illustrates how much our world has changed and the change is due almost entirely to the development of mass communications. So what do we mean by 'mass communication' or 'mass media'? Think of it as the transmission (sending) and reception of 'messages' on a very large scale. Most communication is done on a direct face-to-face basis in a situated cultural context and it is a two-way process. The received message can be responded to instantly. There is 'feedback'.

With mass communication there are four main distinctive features, as follows:

1. There is a gap or an institutional break between the 'sender' of the message and the 'receiver'. The makers of the media texts, the 'senders' of the messages, do not have an obvious feedback relationship with the audience. Audience responses are rarely 'heard'. This means that mass-mediated culture tends to be a one-way process. Producers have to target imaginary, generalised or stereotypical audiences. They can (and do) 'shape' products accordingly. They also make assumptions about audiences that are based on conceptual ideas of what people are like, rather than how they really are. Look at any glamour magazine and you can see what the makers of the texts think men and women should look like, for example.

2. Specialised technologies, especially the internet, have begun to affect the one-way system of communication described above. In addition, these technologies have made it possible to 'capture' messages in a very physical form (photographs, film, tape-recordings) which in turn has led to historical permanence or records. Our sense of 'history' is thus affected (and some would say, constructed.)

3. Media messages can be extended 'outwards', so that events taking place regionally or locally now have global coverage (9/11, for example) Audiences are frequently calculated in billions! This has major significance in terms of media institutions. Lots of profit to be made from selling syndicated rights to the whole world's media!

4. Media messages have therefore become a modern commodity - an industry - a product. Market forces

thus have a definite impact on the production and distribution of media texts. It is argued that as mass media have become 'facts of life' and we have all become socially and culturally more dependent on them.

It is argued that the media now occupy a central role in defining and interpreting the very nature of the world according to certain values, cultural principles and ideologies. We inhabit an information and consumer society as a result and concerns are expressed about exactly what effects the media have on society.

Ideology - a set of ideas or a view of the world that is selective and gives a particular version of reality. Sometimes seen as deliberately constructed by powerful groups in order to maintain power and control.

There are three major areas of concern, as follows:

1. Mass media has a political and a persuasive power over us. Radio, TV, the press and film can manipulate whole societies. Political propaganda, advertising and the so-called 'mind-bending' power of the media are long-standing causes of debate and concern.

2. Since the 19th century there has been a mistrust of so-called 'popular culture', which is thought to debase or degrade cultural traditions and standards. The ongoing debate about the future of public service broadcasting in Britain in the 1990's is an example of this. What exactly is 'quality' and cultural value in broadcast output?

3. The most contentious issue concerns the effects of the mass media on social behaviour, in particular violence and delinquency. The media have regularly been accused of 'causing' outbreaks of unrest in society.

Relations between Culture and Mass Communication

Culture can be defined as the beliefs, values, or other frameworks of reference by which we make sense of our experiences. It also concerns how we communicate these values and ideas. Mass media are centrally involved in the production of modern culture. Media production, media texts and media reception are like a series of interlinked circuits. What is produced is influenced by cultural values; how the texts are formed and represented are influenced in the same way and the readings of the texts are also subject to both abstract and particular cultural viewpoints.

Popular Culture

Historically the term 'popular' was quite a negative thing, with overtones of vulgarity and triviality. Something not 'nice' or 'respectable'. In the modern world, the term means 'widespread', liked or at least encountered by many people. It has also come to mean 'mass-produced', i.e. made for the 'mass' of people. There is a downside to this, of course, in that it can also be interpreted as 'commercial' or 'trashy'. This leads into a further consideration, which is the definition of 'popular culture' as 'low' culture, something not for the elite, but for the 'common' people. Cultural value ('high' culture) has been traditionally associated with dominant or powerful groups - those who have appreciation of classical music, art, ballet, opera and so on. 'Low' or popular culture is everything not approved of as 'high'. It is vulgar, common, or 'easy'.

Another definition of 'popular' is literally 'of the people', a kind of 'folk' culture and this is an interesting area, because it encompasses the idea of an 'alternative' culture which includes minority groups, perhaps with subversive values. The 'indie' music scene is an example of this. So 'popular' culture can and sometimes does, **challenge the 'dominant' cultural power groups.**

Postmodern Culture

It is argued that modern culture has entered a so-called post-modern' phase. Put simply there are four areas of definition here:

1. Because popular culture and media images dominate the age, they dominate our sense of reality. The world is now 'intertextual' (images, copies, simulations and so on are so global that there are no authentic originals any more) The result is that popular culture has replaced art and 'high' culture and the contrived and the simulated has replaced the reality of experience and history. How and what we consume has become more important than what and how we produce.
2. Postmodernism is about style. Pastiche, collage, bricolage (the mixing and re-using of images, signs and symbols) are emphasised at the expense of content or substance.
3. Time, space history and place have become less secure - more confused. The forces of global communications and networks are eroding national cultures. This causes tension and uncertainty.
4. Postmodernism is sceptical about absolute truths, artistic, scientific, historical or political, so a secure sense of time and place is becoming more difficult to sustain. Once secure theories are now open to question and doubt.

The development of the media has had an important influence on private life, the 'withdrawal into inner space' with TV and radio. Leisure activities have been concentrated in the home, although ironically still connected to the outside 'global village'. The media and mass communications have interacted and mixed with pre-existing cultures, forms and values, especially in the development of 'popular culture'.

We are to a large extent dependent on regular contact with the mass media for information, entertainment, ideas, opinion and many other things all of which are connected to our attempts to 'make sense' of who and what we are. Our cultural experiences are affected by the development of systems of mass communication. A look at current research shows that we spend from 18 to 35 hours per week watching TV, for example. It is 'normal' to spend 3 - 4 hours per day in the company of a TV set. Large amounts of our time are spent in a range of media related activities.

Mass Media and Political Culture

Communication is one of the crucial constituents of political life. Some, like the famous German-American Political Scientist Karl W. Deutsche, have even said that politics is nothing but communication. And it is also obvious that incumbents of all different political systems have been well aware of that most of the time. The open question however always has been, what specific function has communication had to fulfill. And in that connection: In what direction was it running- top-down only, in the society itself at the grassroots, bottom-up or more or less symmetrically both ways? Needless to say, these are the very issues even today when it comes to the discussion of the the of mass media in a democracy and for the furtherance of its political culture.

Democracy, usually defined as government by consent, is crucially dependent on a sufficient degree of two-way communication and horizontal communication at the grassroots, otherwise their cannot be consensus building and responsiveness. So, democracy, even in its most modest and reductionism concepts- such as the economic theory of elite competition, requires a free public sphere with a free mass media and certain effective channels for two-way communication, bottom-up and top-down and, what is even more important, open and active deliberations of all issues of public concern. Without this there cannot be democracy worth its name.

In the present era of mass media communication, the old questions are still the key to understanding the contribution of communication to the performance of the political system and its political culture. Mass media, such as newspapers, radio and television do have the potential of including practically everybody into the political public sphere and the process of political deliberation, will formation and decision making.

But, whether they succeed in materializing this historically new potential or not depends on a variety of conditions which by no means are fulfilled automatically once modern mass media come into existence. Print media, Radio and television can cause depoliticization of the rank and file or contribute to its enlightenment and appropriate information, they can serve the sheer interests of political power or that of the population and the public good. Information alone can be quite a mixed blessing. Therefore, a large and crucial portion of the responsibility for both the construction and nutrition of a democratic political culture and even for the long-term performance of governance rests with the media system and its actors. And this is all the more so in the modern media-society as it is here that the media is mainly and sometimes almost the only constituent that can give meaning and structure to the society's public sphere.

Whatever the fruitful contribution of other factors for a of public deliberation, such as civil society, may be in the overall public sphere of modern societies, the responsibility of addressing the supreme decision making bodies and the entire society invariably rests within the reach of the mass media. In this sense, they beat the ultimate responsibility for a quality of public discourse that is democratically adequate.

In present day media democracies, the mass media are a crucial part of their respective political culture contributing substantially to shape the rest of it. For the media to be capable of rising to this challenge, two hard and a whole bunch of soil conditions have to materialize. The most obvious of the hard conditions which normally goes undisputed is of course the legal guarantee for a free media and free flow of information to exist.

An effective legal framework, which gives sufficient protection to the media system and its actors is one of the necessary conditions for a democratic public sphere. Such a legal protection is, as we all know, still far from being even in the post-totalitarian world of today. And, in some countries where the lake appearance of an independent media is stage-managed it is often dangerous to be a responsible journalist.

Conditions for Democratic Communication

In this world, a headway has been made in the right transformation of 1990. With this, one of the hard conditions for democratic communication is being met. But institutional freedom of communication is not yet a sufficient condition for it's appropriate democratic performance. Even formally free media can create a particular type of a representative public sphere which is not much more than a stage on which personal power parades its glory.

The second hard condition to be met lies with the decision-making power over the means of mass communication which normally but not in all cases is connected with the ownership of the different mass media units. This connection, however, is neither direct nor unequivocal. Widespread misunderstanding dominates the discussion.

There are roughly four models of decision-making power connected with the two principal forms of ownership.

a. Public ownership combined with public control over the relevant decisions concerning the performance of the respective media unit.

b. Public ownership combined with government control.

c. Private ownership with decision making at the owners' discretion.

d. Private ownership with decision making in a legal framework or a strong cultural tradition concerning professional rights for journalists, quality standards and the like.

Obviously, some combination of models A and D is required to meet the second hard condition for a public discourse of democratic quality. Many countries today represent one or another type of blend between the different models. In India e.g. there is free press and up till now a government controlled TV. In Germany, you find both public-ally and privately controlled TV and Radio plus private print-media under certain public restrictions for private control.

But even when such a useful model is effective, still certain crucial soft conditions have to be fulfilled for a media system to meet the challenges of democratic communication and democratic culture. As they are often neglected in public discussion we would like to focus our considerations on these additional conditions. They are intrinsically related to the basic structures and functional laws of mass media performance as such and not to the forms of ownership and control alone. Let me just mention some of the most, crucial ones:

1. Mass media are intrinsically asymmetrical. The access to their functions is very unequal. Some social and

political actors do have direct access, others have at least indirect, sometimes even powerful, access and some social actors have no access whatever.

2. Mass media do have the power to set, to build and to shape the political agenda of a polity. Whether political issues at stake in the real political arena and the daily life of society are represented or not in the picture of political life as construed by the media is highly dependent on the media actors who in this respect function as very effective gatekeepers.
3. The agenda structuring function also lies with the media actors as it is up to their discretion whether certain issues rank high or low, are dealt with extensively or in a volatile manner only.
4. But what in the long run may be even more relevant in its effects for building political culture is the way in which the media shape the portrait of the processes and the logic of politics in the political area which is enshrined in the reports they give and in the news they construe.

To cut a complex matter short, we would like to point out some of the most widespread mistakes that are usually made concerning these soft conditions, some of which are most detrimental for an appropriate democratic culture of communication.

Before going into some detail we have however to locate the function of' the mass media system as such in the framework of the entire society. What is the functional role the media system has to perform for the society? Whereas it is the social function of the political system to produce legitimately binding decisions for the whole society, it is the function of the media system to draw the attention of the largest possible part of the society for common issues and by way of that to contribute to the self-perception and integration of a given society.

In order to perform this particular function the media system, of course, cannot follow the same rules of selection, processing and presenting the relevant information as e.g. the educational system or the scientific system. The underlying basic law of the media system is to deal with information in such ways as to maximize attention, however under certain restrictive conditions such as correctness of information, respecting personal, public and private rights and abiding by basic ethical, moral and political standards.

Within the very wide framework constituted by these factors and criteria, media units and media actors are free to construe their picture of political life which under no conditions every can be just the one and only truthful copy of reality. It is invariably a particular construction of reality competing with many other such constructions. Such adequate media constructions are necessarily built through a process of intensive selection and artful presentation. Professionally, in journalism above all, it means competence in the handling of the twin sets of rules of selection and presentation in an appropriate manner. To say it before everything else:

A journalist who desires to audio-educate people just to enlighten, without catching their attention in curiosity, would almost automatically obstruct his very intention to the same degree to which he would abstain from implementing the rules of selection and presentation which are meant to attract attention and which characterize journalistic professionalism.

But in their turn it is also these very same rules which will hamper his efforts for enlightenment if used excessively and without severe controls regarding issues and contexts. Media work means: to attract, to amuse, to entertain and to inform, to explain and may be even to enlighten. Media work is an effort to create accountable forms of synthesis between all these factors.

The immanent tensions between the rules and criteria of successful media presentation of political life entail that the media are amongst the most crucial factors, if they are not the single most and crucial factor which either can contribute positively to the building of a political culture or impede it from emerging and growing.

What if both the hard conditions for free media are met with some dangerous traps for inappropriate performance of media actors along the lines of the soft conditions which is looming large? In some of the most advanced media democracies of the world of today these traps have successfully caught large parts of media performance and, by way of that, impaired their political culture. Let me mention just the most frequent ones.

I. There is above all the fallacy of over-personalization, particularly with respect to political celebrities and incumbents. The fallacy is committed when politics is depicted mainly as an activity of some most prominent political actors. Whatever these actors do is reported as politics. This fallacy suggests itself. Because, at the same time it pleases the mighty and the most prominent figures of the society and caters to the need of large parts of the audience to indulge in a simple, entertaining and fascinating spectacle. In quite a superficial manner, it seems to serve the interests of both sides of the respective media: its consumers because they get a well digestible meal and the mighty which eventually can exercise control over the media and its personnel. However, even in a most autocratic system, politics is always much more than what some of its star actors perform. The dominance of this fallacy in a media system leads to the creation of the representative (feudalistic, pre-democratic) type of public sphere- fascinating power parades.

2. There is also another fallacy closely connected with the first one, the fallacy of just transporting stage-

managed symbolical politics to the audience without making clear what it is by its very nature. Politics invariably has two internally linked dimensions: the instrumental function of problem resolution through policies: for instance, a new school in a village. And, also, it always has the symbolical function of expressing certain meanings and giving sense to an action in a wider socio-political context; for instance, the prime minister coming to that village in order to inaugurate that newly-built school at a public function. However in the world of today, particularly under the influence of mass media (TV), we observe an increasing propensity of political leaders to disconnect the symbolical dimension from the instrumental dimension in most artfully state-managed ways, in many cases, smartly scripted with a well advised view to the media an their rules of functioning. In our case, the prime minister going to that village, richly garlanded, entering a most inappropriate old school and playing, actor-like, the role of a politician highly interested in the progress of the educational systems without delivering anything real.

At least 80 per cent of the media reported activities of Ronald Reagan nave been performed along these lines. In many cases, the placebo character of such symbolical actions is not at all obvious. It is the obligation of quality media not only to mirror the surface of such on-stage activities but also to make transparent their context and background so that its clients get the full and the real information. To the degree in which this fallacy is committed and the stage of the media politics proper will be replaced by a misleading spectacle, which is highly disconnected from the realties of the country.

3. There is the fallacy of following the agenda of the incumbents instead of that of the society. Media actors

of necessity are gatekeepers. It is only for them to take the decisions about their own agenda: what will be in their paper or broadcast and what not. Which issues, persons, problems, ideas, interests, organizations and groups matter and deserve broad attention, urgency or prominence and which don't. Even in very free and professional media systems, there is always a strong propensity of the media to focus on the incumbent, their performance, and the issues they forward, the problems they take serious, and the groups and interest they refer to.

The more modern political communication is shaped and materialized through mass media, the more it becomes true that reality is only what they show it to be. What is not in the media is no! real. To a high degree, therefore, the agenda setting power of' the medic, is' a political decision making power because it defines what can become a matter of political concern and what not. Subsequently, it is one of the most crucial challenges for the media in a democratic society to build .its agenda- the line of interest, problems ideas, hopes amid experiences of the people and the civil society even when they are not delivered and presented in an artful manner on glorious public stages so that the media can swallow and digest them comfortably. The media, which follow the agenda of the power structure, will mainly serve as an echo of the interests and intentions of the powerful.

4. There is the fallacy of depicting politics in an apolitical manner. In a rather exaggerated but interesting way, this fallacy has been analyzed and castigated by the US media ecologist Neil .Postman. According to him, under the predominance of TV-adapted political information strategies, we are about to amuse ourselves ,to death. That means the life and the processes of politics in the mass media of today, more

often than not, is depicted along the lines of drama, amusement, personality clashes, personal charisma, etc. to such a degree that it creates an absolutely distorted picture of what is really going on in politics and leads large portions of the public astray.

Politics in its very substance is a time consuming process in which a broad variety of actors pursue interests and value-based policies using particular resources, refer to public ideals for legitimization, acting in a given institutional and cultural framework. It is invariably not an instant matter but a long term process, with goal attainment or failure through conflict, compromise or consensus and more often that not a mixture of all of them.

These factors and their particular patterns of interaction must become visible and discernable in the media's picture of the political world if it wants to meet its democratic responsibilities. It is the objective of professionalism in journalistic work, at first, to select, to condense, recompose and, secondly, to arrange, stage and give attractive presentational form to political events and topics, but done in such ways that the structure of the what is at stake and where the proper gates and levers for intervention are located. This is no easy art, because the twin traps of either depoliticizing by misusing extensively media forms of presentation of by alienating the audience through instruction methods are always lurking nearby.

Responsibilities of Journalistic Work

The temptation of going the easy ways of either pseudo political entertainment or pseudo communicative political instruction is increased and sometimes overwhelming when one or more or the following three conditions prevail in the contest of journalistic work:

1. lack of professional training and, consequently, of appropriate journalistic skills,
2. pressure from above or outside,
3. extreme shortage of time to be thoroughgoing.

This is why all those responsible for journalistic work, the individual journalists, the journalists' federations, those in charge of the education and training programs for young journalists and those who exercise power over their working conditions and the ways they are made use of have to contribute to favorable conditions for the mass media to perform in such ways as to help democratic political culture to grow.

Because of their wide reach, mass media can contribute immensely to public information and political culture. In a society where literacy rate is still low, it is nonetheless not only radio and TV which provide the rank and file with information and models of understanding and meaning but the print media as well. We know very well from empirical research carried out by the IIMC, each single person in a village that can read a newspaper will spread the news and the schemes of interpretation in a multi-step flow to the rest of the population — provided that the print media are such that at least one of the villagers would he able and like to read it.

Media which obey the rules that can lead to the optimization oft their reach and at the same time carefully mediate politics in an adequate manner and avoid the key fallacies will contribute most substantially to the political culture of democracy both by educating the incumbents and by enlightening the rank and file.

Media which are trapped by the usual fallacies of depoliticizing politics by the way they depict it and build their agenda thus will probably abandon their responsibility blaming everything on the deterioration of' the political culture of their polity.The hard conditions for democratic media communication are necessary but only when the soft factors are also catered for. Thus all 'the sufficient conditions for an appropriate democratic communication are fulfilled. Only then mass media will contribute to the building and development of a democratic political culture that deserves its name.

7

Media and Social Responsibility

A simple model of Corporate Social Responsibility (CSR) starts with the relationship between corporate officers and shareholders. Individuals investing in a firm expect managers to maximize profits. The problems of hidden actions and hidden information give managers some ability to put their own interests ahead of shareholders. One theory of CSR reminds company officials that their primary responsibility is to look after the interests of investors. Another theory of CSR stresses that at times companies impose costs on society without factoring these costs into business calculations. Economists refer to these as negative externalities, since the costs are external to the production decisions of firms.

The CSR movement offers one way to get companies to incorporate their negative effects into firm decision making, such as attempts to get firms to recognize and reduce the impact of their pollution releases. Companies also generate positive spillovers through their operation, such as increases in education, health outcomes, and community development. CSR can be a vehicle to lead firms to produce more of these positive externalities. The preferences of consumers, investors, and workers also give rise to firms' adoption of CSR. Some consumers have preferences over the ways products are generated.

Individuals may care whether fragrances are tested on animals, whether coffee is grown in the shade of tropical forests, and whether chlorine is used in a production process. These consumers create a demand for products that have brand identities associated with concepts such as sustainable development.

Socially conscious investors care about the way profits are generated by a firm. These investors may be willing to trade off some profits for the knowledge that firms they support are less likely to generate negative impacts on society. Companies also use CSR as a way to build and sustain morale. Some firms use CSR as a way to attract and retain workers, with the firm's CSR efforts becoming a signal about the "type" of company it is.

In many countries multinational companies are seen as a resource that can be tapped to solve problems the government is unable or unwilling to tackle. CSR projects in some areas may become part of the price for gaining access to markets. Threats of protest or boycott by NGOs may lead to further expenditures by firms on projects favored by governments or nonprofit advocates. CSR efforts can emerge from efforts by industry to head off stronger government regulations, since firms may prefer the flexibility of selfregulation.If compliance with CSR is less costly for some firms, they may support CSR efforts since this raises rivals' costs.

The multiple definitions of CSR make tracking a company's performance extremely difficult. Conflicts among these theories also raise questions about whether an increase in CSR activities by a firm is necessarily desirable. In the utilitarian framework favored by economists, efforts by firms to maximize profits, reduce negative externalities, or encourage positive externalities will increase social welfare. If CSR actions emerge from government pressure or NGO actions, there may be increases in welfare if firms are led to consider their impact on the environment. Yet there also may be pressures to adopt policies that are inefficient or generate income redistribution at very high costs. These efforts may be politically popular, but they can leave society worse off as measured by the standard of efficiency. Understanding the motivations and impacts of CSR is one of the many challenges faced by journalists who chose to write about this aspect of company performance.

CSR Stories

In his classic work entitled An Economic Theory of Democracy, Anthony Downs identified four different types of information demands that people express. Producers want data that help with their business and production decisions. Consumers want news about prices and quality to help with purchase decisions. People pursue some information simply for entertainment and diversion. Voters and citizens need information to help them make informed choices in politics.

CSR stories contain elements of all four information demands. Managers in some industries follow CSR stories to anticipate how their companies may be affected. Consumers may read about green products or individual investors may search out information on socially conscious investment funds. Reporters aiming to satisfy entertainment demands can frame CSR stories as about human interest, drama, scandal, violence, corruption, or protest. Because CSR stories often revolve around policy issues such as pollution or sustainable development, they also contain elements of public affairs coverage.

To the extent that CSR involves public policy issues, however, coverage will be affected by rational ignorance. Even if individuals care a great deal about sustainable development or social policy, the likelihood their political action will make a difference leads them to remain rationally ignorant about details of these policies. This implies that journalists will not invest in story development or gather the skills necessary to cover policy details. This means that policy stories will be under covered in the press because individuals do not take the time to invest in learning about decisions they cannot influence.

Other characteristics of CSR stories predict they will be less likely to earn space in print and broadcast outlets. In the United States readers and viewers express low interest in international stories. The marginal readers and viewers of U.S. media outlets and the younger demographic set of 18-34 year olds who are highly valued by advertisers are much less likely to express an interest in international stories. The transaction costs of travel and setup costs involved in learning make international news more costly to produce. Lack of corporate transparency raises the costs of accurate reporting for journalists, who find it costly to go beyond company pronouncements in assembling a story about CSR.

The difficulty of quantifying and measuring progress on issues such as the environment, sustainable development, and human rights makes it hard to assess CSR performance, although companies and NGOs are working to develop more accessible CSR indicators. CSR issues often involve concentrated costs (e.g., those borne by the company) and dispersed benefits. The logic of collective action means that beneficiaries may not join together to lobby for CSR changes. Political entrepreneurs and NGOs, who can earn a return in terms of policy change, ideological satisfaction, and fundraising, may represent their interests. Covering the CSR story can involve trying to determine the performance and motivations of NGO actors, which represents an additional challenge for reporters.

Journalists writing about the impact of CSR will find it difficult to assess the impact of company actions. Many corporate efforts are aimed at long-term effects. The causal chain that links a CSR activity with a real-world outcome may be very long, making it difficult to prove whether an effort had the intended effect. Good news will not be news for reporters interested in using an entertainment frame (e.g., scandal, corruption). Editors may simply suspect that corporate ethics is an oxymoron and be reluctant to trust company claims about CSR. The messages from researchers on CSR are mixed. Reporters talking with academics would be hard pressed to determine if CSR is profitable, implemented, driven by altruism or self-interest, or results in improvements in social welfare.

The incentives readers/viewers have to follow CSR stories and the costs facing journalists covering the stories generate predictable patterns in media coverage. Business press outlets will offer articles aimed at satisfying producer and investor information demands. The popular press will focus on entertainment frames in providing CSR stories. Papers such as New York Times, Wall Street Journal, or Financial Times will provide more extensive coverage of policy issues as part of the hard news offerings that differentiate their products.

Development of the Idea of Media's Responsibilities

That the media have a social responsibility to fulfill is certainly not new idea. It was already mentioned by the Hutchins Commission in 1947. Over the past decade the discussion on social responsibility of the media has moved from a rather abstract analysis to more concrete proposals, from a general responsibility idea to concrete mechanisms of accountability, from liability to answerability, while at the same time remaining mainly an academic exercise. Despite this long-standing discussion, one must wonder whether one is asking the right questions, since one cannot define a proper conduct for media unless there is some idea about how the media have an impact on our societies. The political role of the media is an extensively researched mechanism, but probably not the most important. The largest impact of the media is to be found in their cultural role, in the way they change values and norm structures, in the way they influence personal and group identity. These questions have so far not been answered in a definitive manner.

To understand the proper role of the media, one can start from classical sociological analysis about the transition from modern society to its post-modern form as can be found in the work of Beck and Giddens. The clear functional differentiation and role structures that characterized modernity are quickly evaporating. The disappearance of these compartments in society has created new freedom for the individual, but at the same time new problems for identity formation. The individual has lost its unity, is fragmented, differentiated, ambivalent in its many commitments and so forth. Increased personal freedom is therefore at the same time accompanied by increased uncertainty. Value structures are fluctuating so quickly that it is hard for anyone to find solid ground.

But increased personal freedom does not necessarily imply that there is less social control. As Foucault points out in his Surveiller et Punir, the mechanisms of power and control have become much more subtle. Pressure is no longer coming from the outside with strong hierarchical systems, but comes from the inside. Discipline is everywhere, in family structures, schools, organizational life as well as the media. Foucault's analysis squares well with that other sociological tradition routed in the work of Durkheim and Parsons. Both stress that the relation between the world and man is always symbolically mediated and that external control mechanisms are being replaced by forms of internal control: by our feelings, knowledge, beliefs, etc. Because of this evolution, education has become an important variable in sociological explanation. It is of course along these lines that we have to find an explanation for the role and impact of the media. The latter confront the individual with a permanent stream of symbols that mediate our view and understanding of the world. It is beyond doubt one of the most important mechanisms of social control of our times.

A third element that we want to bring up is somewhat less familiar and rests upon the anthropological writings of Mary Douglas who combines elements of Durkheim with the socio-linguistic work of Basil Bernstein. From Emile Durkheim she takes the concept of group pressure, which can be either strong or weak. From Bernstein comes the notion of grid, which stands for the richness of conceptual differentiation that a language allows for e. g., pure/impure, men/women, religious/ profane, and so on. That again can be either weak or strong.

Combining these two dimensions one gets four types of groups. A first group is characterized by a highly diversified conceptual differentiation (lots of grid) and strong social pressure. This is comparable to the hierarchical society of modernity. In these groups personal freedom is very limited. Weak group pressure and weak grid equals great personal freedom and can be connected to the individualistic society of our times.

A third possibility is lots of group pressure, but limited potential for conceptual differentiation. Here we are in an enclavistic group, which relies on strong borderlines between the ins and the outs, those who belong to the group and those who do not. It is also a group that has limited possibility of understanding or explaining the world precisely because the grid is so reduced.

Not so long ago the media discovered the powers of marketing. It proved to be a successful combination, which has become impossible to neglect. One of the techniques used in marketing is to create target groups, a virtual group at which products are aimed. Public broadcasters, newspapers, radio stations and advertisers were all restructured along these virtual group lines. Once one creates a virtual group, one will use all kinds of mechanisms to magnify the group identity, in order to give real people who tune into the group a sense of belonging. An early example of this strategy appearing in Europe is for instance the Dutch TV channel 'TROS,' which presented a completely new style of programming. It is characteristic that after only a few years in operation, the TROS stressed its virtual group identity using slogans such as 'The TROS is there for you'.

With more entertainment and a light-handed presentation of serious topics, TROS introduced the marketing laws that came to dominate the entire media market. By now, virtual groups abound, and recent sociological work has indicated that some of those virtual groups correspond to real groups. That in itself might not be problematic, it is only when one confronts these groups with clearly different pictures of the world on a long term base, that problems can surface. Given the importance of symbolic representation in social control mechanisms today, virtual group structure has at that point turned into a new mechanism of class differentiation. And that is precisely what seems to happen in Flanders between VTM and VRT viewers.

Virtual differentiation has turned into real differentiation and this expresses itself in differences in political sympathies, for instance with respect to migration problems or the attitude towards politicians. Of course it would make no sense at all to presume that it is the media channel itself which has created the real groups;

undoubtedly self-selection plays an important part, but the possibility of a circle setting in which self-selected groups are constantly affirmed in their identity is more than real. Where does all this leave us with respect to media ethics? To put it bluntly, at this point the most important question becomes what is the conceptual richness— the grid— that is offered to the media consumer.

Reduced grid could well turn a virtual group into an enclavistic group that is not very supportive for the society at large. There is some research to corroborate this view. Norris points out that the kind of programs one is watching does matter. Especially light entertainment programs seem to be erosive for civic attitudes. Hooghe finds a clear correlation between sender preference and political preference, but even more between program preference and a general picture of the world. His study corroborates findings by Uslaner, which show that regular watchers of family series have a stronger sense of insecurity. Again, self-selection plays a role, but being caught up in the world of soap opera certainly does not enhance one's view of the world.

What can media regulators do about this? It would seem somewhat odd to scrap all light entertainment from now on, or to put a regulator besides each person forcing him or her to avoid the ultimate soap opera. But there might be other ways, related to media content, that can be helpful. A few years ago the Flemish public broadcaster created the virtual group Radio Donna, characterized by an easy listening profile. However, the news presented at Radio Donna is made by the same team as the one making the news for Radio 1 and it covers the same items. This might seem trivial, but it is not, in terms of grid it is essential that one brings in somewhat of a 'fremdcorper' in order to break reductionist views of the world. This is of course a fine balance; on the one hand a 'fremdcorper' cannot be too strange, otherwise the listener will simply switch. On the other hand, one cannot give in too easily to consumer preference for simple views of the world. The Radio Donna example can be extended to other cases. Each time the central target will be to differentiate the basic picture that is presented in a particular media outlet. One might for instance do this with classical regulation that insists on part of the programs being locally produced, as local programs will often contrast sharply with the standard Hollywood picture of the world. The consumer should at least be given the possibility to take a step back from the virtual group he or she is committed to. On a larger scale, this rule extends to a plea for a strong public broadcaster in each country, as a kind of counterbalance to the dominant commercial media. From this it also follows that if a public broadcaster commercializes too much so that the difference between its programs and that of the commercial counterpart is, this broadcaster loses its very reason for existence. Again, a fine balance will have to be found, and carefully guarded by the controlling authorities.

Media Responsibilities in Time of Elections

The mass media have a range of duties that equally apply to all the media in time of elections: in particular, the duty to prevent misuse of press freedom, to comply with the prescribed timing of election campaign, to duly publish opinion poll findings, etc. At the same time, the legislation sets apart a special class of mass media, which are charged with the heaviest load of responsibilities as regards election campaigns.

Election campaign shall mean the activities of citizens, candidates, electoral associations, electoral blocs, and public associations, which is aimed at encouraging voters to participate in the election and to vote for or against certain candidates.

The mass media does not constitute an independent entity conducting election campaign. However, any entities whose right to do so is recognized by law may conduct such campaign through the media.

One ought to note that election commission members having a full vote, government authorities, bodies of local self-government, charitable organizations, religious associations, persons holding state and municipal offices, government and municipal employees, as well as servicemen are restricted from participation in election campaign when performing their official or service duties or employing any advantages of their office or position. The media are obliged to assure that this prohibition is duly observed.

Conduct of election campaign in the media should fit the same deadlines as those fixed for campaigning if favor of appropriate candidates or lists of candidates proposed by electoral associations or electoral blocs. Election campaign starts from the day when any candidate (list of candidates) is registered, and stops at midnight, 24 hours prior to voting day.

In case of a repeat vote, election campaign resumes from the day when any decision prescribing a repeat vote is officially published and stops at midnight, 24 hours prior to the repeat vote day.

The law expressly provides for time limits as regards election campaign by registered candidates, electoral associations, or electoral blocs via any channels of regulated electronic media. As a rule, such campaign starts after free airtime is apportioned among the candidates, electoral associations, or electoral blocs.

The regulated mass media must allow placement of election commissions' printed information, and must provide election commissions with free airtime in order to advise the voters on the timing and procedure of electoral actions, the progress of election campaign, and the candidates. Any expenses these media incur in such case should be covered from their regular budgetary funds. Other media are obliged to provide the election commissions with necessary information and materials, and to reply to their requests within any time limits prescribed by law. Besides, any acts and resolutions of election commissions adopted within the limits of their jurisdiction are binding on the mass media.

The regulated electronic media are obliged to provide free airtime to registered candidates, electoral associations, and electoral blocs. Provision of free airtime depends of the size of the area covered by the respective medium's TV or radio broadcasts.

A candidate, electoral association, or electoral bloc may independently determine the form and nature of their media campaign, subject to certain exceptions established by law. Thus, the law provides that at least one third of total free airtime allowance shall be provided to candidates, electoral associations, or electoral blocs for holding joint discussions, round table shows, or similar campaign events.

As a rule, free airtime is distributed by a draw of lots held by election commissions in the presence of the candidates, representatives of electoral associations or electoral blocs, and representatives of the respective media organizations. Airtime is apportioned among the candidates, electoral associations or electoral blocs equally, i. e., none of them enjoys any advantage in access to airtime on better terms and conditions (as regards airtime duration, time slot, etc.).

The editors of regulated periodicals circulated in the territory that holds the election are obliged to provide printing space for publication of campaign materials submitted by candidates, electoral associations, or electoral blocs. As a rule, periodicals are understood to include any printed media published at least once a week. The above obligation does not apply to any periodicals established by government authorities and bodies of local self-government with the sole purpose of publishing official communications and materials, regulations and other acts. Specialized publications (for children, on technology, science, etc.) may also be exempted from the obligation to publish printed campaign materials for free, provided they take no part whatsoever in the election campaign.

The minimum total of printing space that a periodical is obliged to provide for free is established by the law governing elections to the respective government authority or any body of local self-government.

Free printing space is provided to candidates, electoral associations, or electoral blocs after such space is apportioned, normally in a draw of lots organized by the respective election commission. All candidates, electoral associations, or electoral blocs participate in this distribution equally.

In case of free publication of campaign materials, the item so published should contain an express reference to the effect that its publication is free, plus an indication as to which candidate, electoral association, or electoral bloc has been so allowed to publish the campaign materials. The candidate, electoral association, or electoral bloc independently determines the form of such publication.

The procedure for free airtime provision somewhat differs between the regulated and other electronic media. The *regulated electronic media* broadcasting in the election territory *.must reserve* pay airtime for election campaign conducted by candidates, electoral associations, or electoral blocs. Such reserved airtime total may not fall below the free airtime total.

Paid airtime should be provided as requested by candidates, electoral associations, or electoral blocs. A contract for provision of pay airtime is made between the regulated medium and respective candidate, electoral association, or electoral bloc. In such case, the payment rate may not be determined separately for each candidate, electoral association, or electoral bloc. There should be a single rate across all candidates, electoral associations, or electoral blocs. The rate should be established in advance and published on or before the day when nomination of candidates (lists of candidates) starts. In case of election pursuant to the majoritarian system, when a constituency map has to be approved, nomination of candidates would normally start on the day when such constituency maps are approved; otherwise, nomination of candidates starts on the day when the election is called. Each candidate has the right to an equal share of paid airtime. The candidate, electoral association, or electoral bloc independently determine the way of utilizing their paid airtime.

Any broadcasters other than the regulated media may provide airtime to candidates, electoral associations, or electoral blocs under contract. In this case, such entities must assure an equal airtime charge, as well as equal terms and conditions of availability (in terms of slot timing and other key parameters) across all candidates, electoral associations, or electoral blocs.

In all cases, regardless of the broadcaster's nature, the airtime shall be paid for only via the campaign funds of respective candidates, electoral associations, or electoral blocs, and such payment must be made in full before the airtime is provided to them. Actual airing time of the pay slot is normally determined in a draw of lots performed by the broadcaster in question.

The regulated periodicals are obliged to provide paid printing space for publication of any materials submitted by candidates, electoral associations, or electoral blocs. The minimum amount of such space is established by the law governing elections to the respective government authority or any body of local self-government:

Unregulated periodicals may provide printing space to candidates, electoral associations, or electoral blocs under a contract. Such publications must assure equal pay rates for the printing space and equal terms and conditions of providing such space (in terms of placement on a page and other key parameters) across all candidates, electoral associations, or electoral blocs. The law establishes only one exception: the requirement of providing printing space on equal terms does not apply to any editors of periodicals, if the periodical in question is founded by any registered candidate, electoral association, electoral bloc, or by any electoral association(s) comprising an electoral bloc.

In all cases, regardless of the publication's nature, the printing space must be paid for only via the campaign funds of respective candidates, electoral associations, or electoral blocs, and such payment must be made in full before the printing space is provided to them. Normally, such printing space is apportioned among the candidates, electoral associations, or electoral blocs in a draw of lots arranged by the respective media organization.

Any material so published in a periodical and paid for from the campaign funds of any candidate, electoral association, or electoral bloc should contain an indication as to which candidate, electoral association, or electoral bloc has drawn on its campaign funds to pay for the publication. The candidate, electoral association, or electoral bloc independently determines the way of utilizing such printing space.

The election legislation establishes a number of special requirements as regards the content of any information published or broadcast by the mass media in the time of elections.

The law establishes some special rules for mass media publication of opinion poll findings, election result forecasts, and other election-related research in the time of elections. When publishing any election-related opinion poll findings, the media must identify the polling organization, the time of poll, the number of those polled (sample size), the method of information gathering, the exact wording of the question, and the statistical estimate of potential error. Within three days to the voting day and on the voting day, no mass media may publish any opinion poll findings, election result forecasts, or other election-related research.

When participating in election campaigns, the regulated media may not allow disclosure (publication) of any information capable of affecting honor, dignity, or business reputation of any candidates, unless the medium in question allows such candidate to issue (publish) a rebuttal or any other clarification as required to protect his or her honor, dignity, or business reputation before the time allocated for election campaign expires.

The election commission that has registered any candidate (list of candidates) should, from time to time, present the mass media with data on receipt and expenditure of money by the campaign funds of any candidates, electoral associations, or electoral blocs, in order to have such information published. The regulated media are obliged to publish the said information within three days of receipt at the expense of their regular funding. Final financial reports of candidates, electoral associations, or electoral blocs are also forwarded to the media for publication.

Any registered candidates working in mass media are relieved of their official duties for as long as they run in the elections. Within three days of their registration, they should provide the election commission with a notarized copy of an appropriate order or directive temporarily relieving them of their official duties. In addition, in their own campaign they may not take any advantage of their office or position. In particular, taking advantage of office or position is understood as priority access to regulated media in order to collect signatures or to conduct election campaign.

Journalists, other creative workers, editorial officials of mass media, as well as officials and creative workers of government broadcasting organizations are restricted from covering the election campaign in the media if the said persons are candidates or agents of any candidates.

Declaration on Fundamental Principles concerning the Contribution of the Mass Media to Strengthening Peace and International Understanding, to the Promotion of Human Rights and to Countering Racialism, Apartheid and Incitement to War

Final text adopted at the 20th session of the General Conference, Paris, October-November 1978 (Unesco document 20C/20 Rev., 21 November 1978

Preamble

The General Conference,

Recalling that by virtue of its Constitution the purpose of Unesco is to 'contribute to peace and security by promoting collaboration among the nations through education, science and culture in order to further universal respect for justice, for the rule of law and for the human rights and fundamental freedoms' (Art I, 1), and that to realize this purpose the Organization will strive 'to promote the free flow of ideas by word and image' (Art I, 2),

Further recalling that under the Constitution the Member States of Unesco, 'believing in full and equal opportunities for education for all, in the unrestricted pursuit of objective truth, and in the free exchange of ideas and knowledge, are agreed and determined to develop and to increase the means of communication between their peoples and to employ these means for the purposes of mutual understanding and a truer and more perfect knowledge of each other's lives' (sixth preambular paragraph),

Recalling the purposes and principles of the United Nations, as specified in its Charter,

Recalling the Universal Declaration of Human Rights, adopted by the General Assembly of the United Nations in 1948 and particularly Article 19 thereof, which provides that everyone has the right to freedom of opinion and expression; this right includes freedom to hold opinions without interference and to seek, receive and impart information and ideas through any media and regardless of frontiers'; and the International Covenant on Civil and Political Rights, adopted by the General Assembly of the United Nations in 1966, Article 19 of which proclaims the same principles and Article 20 of which condemns incitement to war, the advocacy of national, racial or religious hatred and any form of discrimination, hostility or violence

Recalling Article 4 of the International Convention on the Elimination of all Forms of Racial Discrimination, adopted by the General Assembly of the United Nations in 196j, and the International Convention on the Suppression and Punishment of the Crime of Apartheid, adopted by the General Assembly of the United Nations in 1973, whereby the States acceding to these Conventions under-took to adopt immediate and positive measures designed to eradicate all incitement to, or acts of, racial discrimination, and agreed to prevent any encouragement of the crime of apartheid and similar segregationist policies or their manifestations,

Recalling the Declaration on the Promotion among Youth of the Ideals of Peace, Mutual Respect and Understanding between Peoples, adopted by the General Assembly of the United Nations in 1965,

Recalling the declarations and resolutions adopted by the various organs of the United Nations concerning the establishment of a new international economic order and the role Unesco is called upon to play in this respect,

Recalling the Declaration of the Principles of International Cultural Cooperation, adopted by the General Conference of Unesco in 1966,

Recalling Resolution 59(1) of the General Assembly of the United Nations, adopted in 1946 and declaring:

'Freedom of information is a fundamental human right and is the touchstone of all the freedoms to which the United Nations is consecrated;

Freedom of information requires as an indispensable element the willingness and capacity to employ its privileges without abuse. It requires as a basic discipline the moral obligation to seek the facts without prejudice and to spread knowledge without malicious intent;

Recalling Resolution 110(11) of the General Assembly of the United Nations, adopted in 1947, condemning all forms of propaganda which are designed or likely to provoke or encourage any threat to the peace, breach of the peace, or act of aggression,

Recalling resolution 127(11), also adopted by the General Assembly in 1947 which invites Member States to take measures, within the limits of constitutional procedures, to combat the diffusion of false or distorted reports likely to injure friendly relations between States, as well as the other resolutions of the General Assembly concerning the mass media and their contribution to strengthening peace, trust and friendly relations among States,

Recalling resolution 9.12 adopted by the General Conference of Unesco in 1968, reiterating Unesco's objective to help to eradicate colonialism and racialism, and resolution 12.1 adopted by the General Conference in 1976, which proclaims that colonialism, neo-colonialism and racialism in all its forms and manifestations are incompatible with the fundamental aims of Unesco,

Recalling resolution 4.301 adopted in 1970 by the General Conference of Unesco on the contribution of the information media to furthering international understanding and co-operation in the interests of peace and human welfare, and to countering propaganda on behalf of war, racialism, apartheid and hatred among nations, and aware of the fundamental contribution that mass media can make to the realizations of these objectives,

Recalling the Declaration on Race and Racial Prejudice adopted by the General Conference of Unesco at its twentieth session,

Conscious of the complexity of the problems of information in modern society, of the diversity of solutions which have been offered to them, as evidenced in particular by the consideration given to them within Unesco, and of the legitimate desire of all parties concerned that their aspirations, points of view and cultural identity be taken into due consideration,

Conscious of the aspirations of the developing countries for the establishment of a new, more just and more effective world information and communication order,

Proclaims on this twenty-eighth day of November 1978 this Declaration on Fundamental Principles concerning the Contribution of the Mass Media to strengthening Peace and International Understanding, to the Promotion of Human Rights and to Countering Racialism, Apartheid and Incitement to War.

Article I

The strengthening of peace and international understanding, the promotion of human rights and the countering of racialism, apartheid and incitement to war demand a free flow and a wider and better balanced dissemination of information. To this end, the mass media have a leading contribution to make. This contribution will be the more effective to the extent that the information reflects the different aspects of the subject dealt with.

Article II

The exercise of freedom of opinion, expression and information recognized as an integral part of human rights and fundamental freedoms, is a vital factor in the strengthening of peace and international understanding.

Access by the public to information should be guaranteed by the diversity of the sources and means of information available to it, thus enabling each individual to check the accuracy of facts and to appraise events objectively. To this end, journalists must have freedom to report and the fullest possible facilities of access to information. Similarly, it is important that the mass media be responsive to concerns of peoples and individuals, thus promoting the participation of the public in the elaboration of information

With a view to the strengthening of peace and international understanding, to promoting human rights and to countering racialism, apartheid and incitement to war, the mass media throughout the world, by reason of their role, contribute to promoting human rights, in particular by giving expression to oppressed peoples who struggle against colonialism neo-colonialism foreign occupation and all forms of racial discrimination and oppression and who are unable to make their voices heard within their own territories.

If the mass media are to be in a position to promote the principles of this Declaration in their activities, it is essential that journalists and other agents of the mass media, in their own country or abroad, be assured of protection guaranteeing them the best conditions for the exercise of their profession.

Article III

The Mass media have an important contribution to make to the strengthening of peace and international understanding and in countering racialism, apartheid and incitement to war.

In countering aggressive war, racialism, apartheid and other violations of human rights which are *inter alia* spawned by prejudice and ignorance, the mass media, by disseminating information on the aims, aspiration, cultures and needs of all peoples, contribute to eliminate ignorance and misunderstanding between peoples, to make nationals of a country sensitive to the needs and desires of others, to ensure the respect of the rights and dignity of all nations, all peoples and all individuals without distinction of race, sex, language, religion or nationality and to draw attention to the great evils which afflict humanity, such as poverty, malnutrition and diseases, thereby promoting the formulation by States of the policies best able to promote the reduction of international tension and the peaceful and equitable settlement of international disputes.

Article IV

The mass media have an essential part to play in the education of young people in a spirit of peace, justice, freedom, mutual respect and understanding, in order to promote human rights, equality of rights as between all human beings and all nations, and economic and social progress. Equally, they have an important role to play in making known the views and aspirations of the younger generation.

Article V

In order to respect freedom of opinion, expression and information and in order that information may reflect all points of view, it is important that the points of view presented by those who consider that the information published or disseminated about them has seriously prejudiced their effort to strengthen peace and international understanding, to promote human rights or to counter racialism, apartheid and incitement to war be disseminated.

Article VI

For the establishment of a new equilibrium and greater reciprocity in the flow of information, which will be conducive to the institution of a just and lasting peace and to the economic and political independence of the developing countries, it is necessary to correct the inequalities in the flow of information to and from developing countries, and between those countries. To this end, it is essential that their mass media should have conditions and resources enabling them to gain strength and expand, and to co-operate both among themselves and with the mass media in developed countries.

Article VII

By disseminating more widely all of the information concerning the universally accepted objectives and principles which are the bases of the resolutions adopted by the different organs of the United Nations, the mass media contribute effectively to the strengthening of peace and international understanding, to the promotion of human rights, and to the establishment of a more just and equitable international economic order.

Professional organizations, and people who participate in the professional training of journalists and other agents of the mass media and who assist them in performing their functions in a responsible manner should attach special importance to the principles of this Declaration when drawing up and ensuring application of their codes of ethics.

Article IX

In the spirit of this Declaration, it is for the international community to contribute to the creation of the conditions for a free flow and wider and more balanced dissemination of information, and of the conditions for the protection, in the exercise of their functions, of journalists and other agents of the mass media. Unesco is well placed to make a valuable contribution in this respect.

Article X

With due respect for constitutional provisions designed to guarantee freedom of information and for the applicable international instruments and agreements, it is indispensable to create and maintain throughout the world the conditions which make it possible for the organizations and persons professionally involved in the dissemination of information to achieve the objectives of this Declaration.

It is important that a free flow and wider and better balanced dissemination of information be encouraged.

To this end, it is necessary that States facilitate the procurement by the mass media in the developing countries of adequate conditions and resources enabling them to gain strength and expand, and that they support co-operation by the latter both among themselves and with the mass media in developed countries.

Similarly, on a basis of equality of rights, mutual advantage and respect for the diversity of the cultures which go to make up the common heritage of mankind, it is essential that bilateral and multilateral exchanges of information among all States, and in particular between those which have different economic and social systems, be encouraged and developed.

Article XI

For this declaration to be fully effective it is necessary, with due respect for the legislative and administrative provisions and the other obligations of Member States, to guarantee the existence of favourable conditions for the operation of the mass media, in conformity with the provisions of the Universal Declaration of Human Rights and with the corresponding principles proclaimed in the International Covenant on Civil and Political Rights adopted by the General Assembly of the United Nations in 1966.

8

Traditional Mass Media

NEWSPAPERS

A newspaper is a lightweight and disposable publication, usually printed on low-cost paper called newsprint. It may be general or special interest, and may be published daily, weekly, biweekly, monthly, bimonthly, or quarterly. General-interest newspapers are usually journals of current news on a variety of topics. Those can include political events, crime, business, sports, and opinions. Many also include weather news and forecasts. Newspapers increasingly use photographs to illustrate stories; they also often include comic strips and other entertainment, such as crosswords. The general variety is issued every day (a daily newspaper), often with the exception of Sundays and some national holidays. Weekly newspapers, printed once a week, are also common; they tend to be smaller and less prestigious than daily papers.

Most nations have at least one newspaper that circulates throughout the whole country: a national newspaper, as contrasted with a local newspaper serving a city or region. In the United States and Canada, there are few truly national newspapers, with the notable exceptions of USA Today in the United States and The Globe and Mail and The National Post in Canada. Large metropolitan newspapers with expanded distribution networks such as The New York Times, The Washington Post, and The Toronto Star can fill the role of de facto national newspapers. The owner of the newspaper, or person in charge, is the publisher. The person responsible for content is the editor, editor in chief, or executive editor.

Newspapers have been developed around very narrow topic areas, such as news for merchants in a specific industry, fans of particular sports, fans of the arts or of specific artists, and participants in the same sorts of activities or lifestyles.

Most modern newspapers are in one of three sizes:

— broadsheets (29½ by 23½ inches, or about 749 by 597 mm), generally associated with more intellectual newspapers.

— tabloids: half the size of broadsheets, and often seen as sensationalist in contrast to them.

— Berliner or midi (470×315 mm), used by European papers such as Le Monde.

They are usually printed on a thin, somewhat rough, off-white coloured paper known as newsprint. Since the 1980s, many newspapers have been printed with three-color process photography and graphics. This highlights the fact that the layout of the newspaper is of major importance in getting attention so readers will see and enjoy large sections of the newspaper.To help their titles stand out on the newsstands, some newspapers are not printed on conventional off-white coloured newsprint.

The number of copies sold on an average day is called the newspaper's circulation, and is used to set advertising rates.

According to United Nations data from 1995 Japan has three daily papers with a circulation well above 4 million. Germany's Bild, with a circulation of 4.5 million, was the only other paper in that category. In the United Kingdom The Sun is the top seller, with around 3.2 million copies distributed daily (late-2004). In India, The Times of India is the largest English newspaper with 2.14 million copies daily. In the United States and the United Kingdom at least, circulation has been declining for many years.

USA Today has daily circulation of approximately 2 million, making it the most widely distributed paper in the country. However, the validity of USA Today's circulation figures are disputed by some in the newspaper community. This is because of the newspaper's contracts with hotels. Many of its papers are delivered to hotel guests who do not realise they are being charged for it.

Business Side of Newspapers

Almost all newspapers make nearly all their money from advertising. The income from the customer's payment at the newsstand is a pittance in comparison. That is why all newspapers cost little and some are free. The portion of the newspaper that is not advertising is called editorial content or editorial matter.

Publishers of commercial newspapers strive for higher circulation so that advertising in their newspaper becomes more effective, allowing the newspaper to attract more advertisers and charge more for the service. But some advertising sales also market demographics: Some newspapers might sacrifice higher circulation numbers in favor of an audience with a higher income. Many paid-for newspapers offer a variety of subscription plans. For example, someone might only want a Sunday paper, or perhaps only Sunday and Saturday, or maybe only a workweek subscription, or perhaps a daily subscription.

Some newspapers provide some or all of their content on the Internet, either at no cost or for a fee. In some cases free access is only available for a matter of days or weeks, or readers must register and provide personal data. In other cases, extensive free archives are provided.

Newspaper Journalism

Since newspapers began as a journal (record of current events), the profession involved in the making of newspapers began to be called journalism. Much emphasis has been placed upon the value of the journalist to be accurate and fair in the historical record.

In the yellow journalism era of the 19th century, many newspapers in the United States relied on sensational stories that were meant to anger or excite the public, rather than to inform. The more restrained style of reporting that relies on fact checking and accuracy regained popularity around World War II.

Criticism of journalism is varied and sometimes vehement. Charges of sensationalism have diminished to a degree. But credibility is questioned because of anonymous sources; errors in facts, spelling, and grammar; real or perceived bias; and scandals involving plagiarism and fabrication.

In the past newspapers have often been owned by so-called press barons, and were used either as a rich man's toy, or used as a political tool. More recently in the United States, a greater number of newspapers (and all of the largest ones) are being run by large media corporations such as Gannett (the largest in the United States) Cox, The Tribune Company, etc. Many industry watchers have concerns that the growing need for profit growth natural to corporations will have a negative impact on the overall quality of journalism.

Even though the opinions of the owners are often relegated to the editorial section, and the opinions of the readers are in the op-ed ("opposite the editorial page") and letters to the editors sections of the paper, newspapers have been used for political purposes by insinuating some kind of bias outside of the editorial section and into straight news. For example, The New York Times is often criticised for a leftist slant to its stories, or, by others, for supporting the American political establishment in nearly all cases, whereas The Wall Street Journal has a history of emphasising the position of the right.

Some ways newspapers have tried to improve their credibility are: appointing ombudsmen, developing ethics policies and training, using more stringent corrections policies, communicating their processes and rationale with readers, and asking sources to review articles after publication. Many larger newspapers are now using more aggressive random fact-checking to further improve the chances that false information will be found before it is printed.

Future of Newspapers

The future of newspapers is cloudy, with overall readership slowly declining in most developed countries due to increasing competition from television and the Internet. The 57th annual World Newspaper Congress, held in Istanbul in June 2004, reported circulation increases in only 35 of 208 countries studied. Most of the increase came in developing countries, notably China.

A report at the gathering said China tops total newspaper circulation, with more than 85 million copies of papers sold every day, followed by India with 72 million—China and India are the two most populous countries in the world—followed by Japan with 70 million and the United States with 55 million. The report said circulation declined by an average of 2.2 percent across 13 of the 15 countries that made up the European Union before May 1. The biggest declines were in Ireland, down

7.8 percent; Britain, down 4.7 percent; and Portugal, where numbers fell by 4.0 percent. One growth area is the distribution of free newspapers, which are not reflected in the above circulation data. They grew 16 percent in 2003.

Another growth area is high-quality tabloids, particularly in the UK, where several of the major broadsheets are experimenting with the format. Smaller and easier to hold than broadsheets, but presenting real journalism rather than traditional tabloid fodder, they appear to have drawn some younger readers who are otherwise abandoning newspapers. Newspapers also face increased competition from the Internet for classified ads, especially for jobs, which have long been a key source of revenue.

MAGAZINES

Magazines are periodical publications containing a variety of articles on various subjects. They are typically published weekly, biweekly, monthly, or quarterly, with a date on the cover that is in advance of the date it is actually published. They are often printed in color on coated paper.

Magazines usually have articles on popular topics of interest to the general public and are written at the reading level of most of the population. An academic periodical featuring scholarly articles written in a more specialist register is usually called a "journal." "Periodical" is the word usually used to describe magazines, journals, newspapers, newsletters, and anything else that is published in regular intervals for an indefinite period of time, but "serial" is sometimes used, especially in librarianship.

Many weekend newspapers incorporate magazine supplements, such as Parade; the Times Literary Supplement, and LIFE in its most recent incarnation.

The Gentleman's Magazine, first published in 1731, is considered to be the first general-interest magazine. The oldest magazine still in print is The Scots Magazine, which was first published in 1739, though multiple changes in ownership and gaps in publication totaling over 90 years weaken that claim.

The most widely distributed magazine in the world is Reader's Digest (founded in 1922). Its worldwide circulation including all editions comprises 21 million copies and over 100 million readers. The Watchtower is the most widely distributed religious magazine in the world, with an average circulation of 26.4 million copies semimonthly in more than 150 languages.

Radio

Radio is the wireless transmission of signals, by modulation of electromagnetic waves with frequencies below those of light. Radio waves are a form of electromagnetic radiation, created whenever a charged object accelerates with a frequency that lies in the radio frequency (RF) portion of the electromagnetic spectrum. This is the range from a few tens of hertz to a few hundred gigahertz. Electromagnetic radiation travels (propagates) by means of oscillating electric and magnetic fields that pass through the air and the vacuum of space equally well, and does not require a medium of transport.

Other types of electromagnetic radiation, with frequencies above the RF range are infrared, visible light, ultraviolet,X-rays and gamma rays. Since the energy of an individual photon of radio frequency is too low to remove an electron from an atom, radio waves are classified as non-ionizing radiation. When radio waves pass a wire, their oscillating electric or magnetic field (depending on the shape of the wire) induces an alternating current and voltage in the wire. This can be transformed into audio or other signals that carry information. Although the word 'radio' is used to describe this phenomenon, the transmissions which we know as television, radio, radar, and cell phone are all in the class of radio frequency emissions.

The theoretical basis of the propagation of electromagnetic waves was first described in 1873 by James Clerk Maxwell in his paper to the Royal Society A dynamical theory of the electromagnetic field, which followed his work between 1861 and 1865.

In 1878 David E. Hughes was the first to transmit and receive radio waves when he noticed that his induction balance caused noise in the receiver of his homemade telephone. He demonstrated his discovery to the Royal Society in 1880 but was told it was merely induction.

It was Heinrich Rudolf Hertz who, between 1886 and 1888, first validated Maxwell's theory through experiment, demonstrating that radio radiation had all the properties of waves (now called Hertzian waves), and discovering that the electromagnetic equations could be reformulated into a partial differential equation called the wave equation.

The identity of the original inventor of radio, at the time called wireless telegraphy, is contentious. Claims have been made that Nathan Stubblefield invented radio before either Nikola Tesla or Guglielmo Marconi, but his device seems to have worked by induction transmission rather than radio transmission.

In 1893 in St. Louis, Missouri, Tesla made the first public demonstration of radio communication. Addressing the Franklin Institute in Philadelphia and the National Electric Light Association, he described and demonstrated in detail the principles of radio communication. The apparatus that he used contained all the elements that were incorporated into radio systems before the development of the vacuum tube. He initially used magnetic receivers, unlike the coherers used by Marconi and other early experimenters.

On 19 August 1894, British physicist Sir Oliver Lodge demonstrated the reception of Morse code signalling using radio waves using a detecting device called a coherer, a tube filled with iron filings which had been invented by Temistocle Calzecchi-Onesti at Fermo in Italy in 1884. Edouard Branly of France and Alexander Popov of Russia later produced improved versions of the coherer. Popov, who was the first to develop a practical communication system based on the coherer, is usually considered by his own countrymen to have been the inventor of radio. The Indian physicist, Jagdish Chandra Bose, demonstrated publicly the use of radio waves in November of 1894 in Calcutta, but he was not interested in patenting his work.

In 1896 Marconi was awarded what is sometimes recognised as the world's first patent for radio with British Patent 12039, Improvements in transmitting electrical impulses and signals and in apparatus there-for. In 1897 he established the world's first radio station on the Isle of Wight, England. The same year in the U.S., some key developments in radio's early history were created and patented by Tesla. The U.S. Patent Office reversed its decision in 1904, awarding Marconi a patent for the invention of radio, possibly influenced by Marconi's financial backers in the States, who included Thomas Edison and Andrew Carnegie. Some believe this was made for financial reasons, allowing the U.S. government to avoid having to pay the royalties that were being claimed by Tesla for use of his patents.

In 1909, Marconi, with Karl Ferdinand Braun, was also awarded the Nobel Prize in Physics for "contributions to the development of wireless telegraphy". However, Tesla's patent was reinstated in 1943 by the U.S. Supreme

Court, shortly after his death. This decision was based on the fact that prior art existed before the establishment of Marconi's patent. Some believe the decision was also made for financial reasons, to allow the U.S. government to avoid having to pay damages that were being claimed by the Marconi Company for use of its patents during World War I.

Marconi opened the world's first "wireless" factory in Hall Street, Chelmsford, England in 1898, employing around 50 people. Around 1900, Tesla opened the Wardenclyffe Tower facility and advertised services. By 1903, the tower structure neared completion. Various theories exist on how Tesla intended to achieve the goals of this wireless system. Tesla claimed that Wardenclyffe, as part of a World System of transmitters, would have allowed secure multichannel transceiving of information, universal navigation, time synchronization, and a global location system.

Wireless signals proved effective in communication for rescue work when a sea disaster occurred. Effective communication was able to exist between ships and ship to shore points. A number of ocean liners installed wireless equipment. In 1899 the United States Army established wireless communications with a lightship off Fire Island, New York. Two years later the Navy adopted a wireless system. Up to then, the Navy had been using visual signaling and homing pigeons for communication.

In 1901, radiotelegraph service was instituted between five Hawaiian Islands. By 1903, a Marconi station located in Wellfleet, Massachusetts, carried an exchange or greetings between President Theodore Roosevelt and King Edward VII. In 1905 the naval battle of Port Arthur in the Russo-Japanese war was reported by wireless, and in 1906 the U.S. Weather Bureau experimented with radiotelegraphy to speed notice of weather conditions.

In 1909, Robert E. Peary, arctic explorer, radiotelegraphed: "I found the Pole". In 1910 Marconi opened regular American-European radiotelegraph service, which several months later, enabled an escaped British murderer to be apprehended on the high seas. In 1912, the first transpacific radiotelegraph service linked San Francisco with Hawaii.

Overseas radiotelegraph service developed slowly, primarily because the initial radiotelegraph set discharged electricity within the circuit and between the electrodes was unstable causing a high amount of interference. The Alexanderson high-frequency alternator and the De Forest tube resolved many of these early technical problems. The Navy made major use of radio transmitters — especially Alexanderson alternators, the only reliable long-distance wireless transmitters - for the duration.

During World War I, governments began using radiotelegraph to be alert of events and to instruct the movement of troops and supplies. World War II demonstrated the value of radio and spurred its development and later utilization for peacetime purposes. Radiotelegraph circuits to other countries enabled persons almost anywhere in the United States to communicate with practically any place on earth.

Since 1923, pictures have been transmitted by wire, when a photograph was sent from Washington to Baltimore in a test. The first transatlantic radiophoto relay came in 1924 when the Radio Corporation of America beamed a picture of Charles Evans Hughes from London to New York. RCA inaugurated regular radiophoto service in 1926.

Two radio communication companies once had domestic networks connecting certain large cities, but these were closed in World War II. However, microwave and other developments have made it possible for domestic telegraph communication to be carried largely in part over radio circuits. In 1945 Western Union established the first microwave beam system, connecting New York and Philadelphia. This has since been extended and is being developed into a coast-to-coast system. By 1988 Western Union could transmit about 2,000 telegrams simultaneously in each direction.

The first time the human voice was transmitted by radio is debateable. Claims to that distinction range from the phase, "Hello Rainey" spoken by Natan B. Stubblefield to a test partner near Murray, Kentucky, in 1892, to an experimental program of talk and music by Reginald A. Fessenden, of Brant Rock, Massachusetts, in 1906, which was heard by radio-equipped ships within several hundred miles.

In 1915 speech was first transmitted across the continent from New York City to San Francisco and across the Atlantic Ocean from Naval radio station NAA at Arlington, Virginia, to the Eiffel Tower in Paris. There was some experimental military radiotelephony in World War I between ground and aircraft.

The first ship-to-shore two way radio conversation occurred in 1922, between Deal Beach, New Jersey, and the S.S. America, 400 miles at sea. However, it was not until 1929 that high seas public radiotelephone service was inaugurated. At that time telephone contact could be made only with ships within 1,500 miles of shore. Today there is the ability to telephone nearly every large ship wherever it may be on the globe.

Commercial radiotelephony linking North America with Europe was opened in 1927, and with South America three years later. In 1935 the first telephone call was made around the world, using a combination of wire and radio circuits. Until 1936, all American transatlantic telephone communication had to be routed through England. In that year, a direct radiotelephone circuit was opened to Paris. Telephone connection by radio and cable is now accessible with 187 foreign points.

Uses of Radio

Many of radio's early uses were maritime, for sending telegraphic messages using Morse code between ships and land. One of the earliest users included the Japanese Navy scouting the Russian fleet during the Battle of Tsushima in 1901. One of the most memorable uses of marine telegraphy was during the sinking of the RMS Titanic in 1912, including communications between operators on the sinking ship and nearby vessels, and communications to shore stations listing the survivors.

Radio was used to pass on orders and communications between armies and navies on both sides in World War I; Germany used radio communications for diplomatic messages once its submarine cables were cut by the British. The United States passed on President Woodrow Wilson's Fourteen Points to Germany via radio during the war.

Broadcasting began to become feasible in the 1920s, with the widespread introduction of radio receivers, particularly in Europe and the United States. Besides broadcasting, point-to-point broadcasting, including telephone messages and relays of radio programs, became widespread in the 1920s and 1930s.

Another use of radio in the pre-war years was the development of detecting and locating aircraft and ships by the use of radar. Today, radio takes many forms, including wireless networks, mobile communications of all types, as well as radio broadcasting. Read more about radio's history. Before the advent of television, commercial radio broadcasts included not only news and music, but dramas, comedies, variety shows, and many other forms of entertainment. Radio was unique among dramatic presentation that it used only sound.

There are a number of uses of radio:

— AM broadcast radio sends music and voice in the Medium Frequency (MF — 0.300 MHz to 3 MHz) radio spectrum. AM radio uses amplitude modulation, in which louder sounds at the microphone causes wider fluctuations in the transmitter power while the transmitter frequency remains unchanged. Transmissions are affected by static because lightning and other sources of radio add their radio waves to the ones from the transmitter.

— FM broadcast radio sends music and voice, with higher fidelity than AM radio. In frequency modulation, louder sounds at the microphone cause the transmitter frequency to fluctuate farther, the transmitter power stays constant. FM is transmitted in the Very High Frequency (VHF — 30 MHz to 300 MHz) radio spectrum. FM requires more radio frequency space than AM and there are more frequencies available at higher frequencies, so there can be more stations, each sending more information. Another effect is that shorter VHF radio waves act more like light, travelling in straight lines, hence the reception range is generally limited to about 50-100 miles. During unusual upper atmospheric conditions, FM signals are occasionally reflected back towards the Earth by the ionosphere, resulting in Long distance FM reception. FM receivers are subject to the capture effect, which causes the radio to only receive the strongest signal when multiple signals appear on the same frequency. FM receivers are relatively immune to lightning and spark interference.

— FM Subcarrier services are secondary signals transmitted "piggyback" along with the main program. Special receivers are required to utilize these services. Analog channels may contain alternative programming, such as reading services for the blind, background music or stereo sound signals. In some extremely crowded metropolitan areas, the subchannel program might be an alternate foreign language radio program for various ethnic groups. Subcarriers can also transmit digital data, such as station identification, the current song's name, web addresses, or stock quotes. In some countries, FM radios automatically retune themselves to the same channel in a different district by using sub-bands.

— Aviation voice radios use VHF AM. AM is used so that multiple stations on the same channel can be received. (Use of FM would result in stronger stations blocking out reception of weaker stations due to FM's capture effect). Aircraft fly high enough that their transmitters can be received hundreds of miles (kilometres) away, even though they are using VHF.

— Marine voice radios can use AM in the shortwave High Frequency (HF — 3 MHz to 30 MHz) radio spectrum for very long ranges or narrowband FM in the VHF spectrum for much shorter ranges.

— Government, police, fire and commercial voice services use narrowband FM on special frequencies. Fidelity is sacrificed to use a smaller range of radio frequencies, usually five kilohertz of deviation (5 thousand cycles per second), rather than the 75 used by FM broadcasts and 25 used by TV sound.

— Civil and military HF (high frequency) voice services use shortwave radio to contact ships at sea, aircraft and isolated settlements. Most use single sideband voice (SSB), which uses less bandwidth than AM. SSB sounds like ducks quacking on an AM radio. Viewed as a graph of frequency versus power, an AM signal shows power where the frequencies of the voice add and subtract with the main radio frequency. SSB cuts the bandwidth in half by suppressing the carrier and (usually) lower sideband.

— TETRA, Terrestrial Trunked Radio is a digital cell phone system for military, police and ambulances.

— Commercial services such as XM and Sirius offer digital Satellite radio.

Digital Radio

The oldest form of digital broadcast was spark gap telegraphy, used by pioneers such as Marconi. By pressing the key, the operator could send messages in Morse code by energizing a rotating commutating spark gap. The rotating commutator produced a tone in the receiver, where a simple spark gap would produce a hiss, indistinguishable from static. Spark gap transmitters are now illegal, because their transmissions span several hundred megahertz. This is very wasteful of both radio frequencies and power.

The next advance was continuous wave telegraphy, or CW, in which a pure radio frequency, produced by a vacuum tube lectronic oscillator was switched on and off by a key. A receiver with a local oscillator would "heterodyne" with the pure radio frequency, creating a whistle-like audio tone. CW uses less than 100Hz of bandwidth. CW is still used, these days primarily by amateur radio operators (hams). Strictly, on-off keying of a carrier should be known as "Interrupted Continuous Wave" or ICW.

Radio teletypes usually operate on short-wave (HF) and are much loved by the military because they create written information without a skilled operator. They send a bit as one of two tones. Groups of five or seven bits become a character printed by a teletype. From about 1925 to 1975, radio teletype was how most commercial messages were sent to less developed countries. These are still used by the military and weather services. Aircraft use a 1200 Baud radioteletype service over VHF to send their ID, altitude and position, and get gate and connecting-flight data.

Microwave dishes on satellites, telephone exchanges and TV stations usually use quadrature amplitude modulation (QAM). QAM sends data by changing both the phase and the amplitude of the radio signal. Engineers like QAM because it packs the most bits into a radio signal. Usually the bits are sent in "frames" that repeat. A special bit pattern is used to locate the beginning of a frame. IEEE 802.11, the radio network standard, has stations with digital tuners. They start off by contacting a central control node, which tells the nodes about each other so they can communicate privately. Nodes move through many frequencies. They use a pseudo-random number generator to select the next frequency.

FILM

Film is a term that encompasses motion pictures as individual projects, as well as the field in general. The origin of the name comes from the fact that photographic film has historically been the primary medium for recording and displaying motion pictures. Many other terms exist — motion pictures, the silver screen, photoplays, picture shows, flicks — and most commonly movies. Academics and the English-speaking international community prefer to use film or "cinema", due to the colloquial nature of these other terms.

Films are produced by recording actual people and objects with cameras, or by creating them using animation techniques and/or special effects. They comprise a series of individual frames, but when these images are shown rapidly in succession, the illusion of motion is given to the viewer. Flickering between frames is not seen due to an effect known as persistence of vision — whereby the eye retains a visual image for a fraction of a second after the source has been removed. Perhaps of more relevance is what causes the perception of motion — a psychological effect identified as beta movement.

Film is considered by many to be an important art form; films entertain, educate, enlighten and inspire audiences. The visual elements of cinema need no translation, giving the motion picture a universal power of communication. Any film can become a worldwide attraction, especially with the addition of dubbing or subtitles that translate the dialogue. Films are also artifacts created by specific cultures, which reflect those cultures and, in turn, affect them.

History of Film

Mechanisms for producing artificially created, two-dimensional images in motion were demonstrated as early as the 1860's, including the zoetrope and the praxinoscope. These machines were outgrowths of simple optical devices (such as magic lanterns), and would display sequences of still pictures at sufficient speed for the images on the pictures to appear to be moving. Naturally, the images needed to be carefully designed to achieve the desired effect — and the underlying principle became the basis for the development of animation.

With the development of celluloid film for still photography, it became possible to directly capture objects in motion in real time using the new medium. Early versions of the technology sometimes required the viewer to look into a special device to see the pictures. By the 1880's, the development of the motion picture camera allowed the individual component images to be captured and stored on a single reel, and led quickly to the development of a motion picture projector to shine light through the processed and printed film and magnify these "moving picture shows" onto a screen for an entire audience. These reels, so exhibited, came to be known as motion pictures".

Motion pictures were purely visual art up to the late 1920s, but these innovative silent films had gained a hold on the public imagination. When films began to tell stories, instead of just record brief events, exhibitors sometimes provided a commentator to narrate the action, but this became unnecessary with the development of printed intertitles containing the actors' dialogue and other written, descriptive material as part of the visual experience. Rather than leave the audience in silence, theater owners would hire a pianist or organist or a full orchestra to play music fitting the mood of the film at any given moment. By the early 1920s, most films came with a prepared list of sheet music for this purposes, with complete film scores being composed for major productions.

In the late 1920s, technology allowed filmmakers to attach to each film a soundtrack of speech, music and sound effects synchronized with the action on the screen, these sound films were initially distinguished by calling them "talking pictures", or talkies.

The next major step in the development of cinema was the introduction of color. While the addition of sound quickly eclipsed silent film and theater musicians, color was adopted more gradually. The public was relatively indifferent to color photography as opposed to black-and-white. But as color processes improved and became as affordable as black-and-white film, more and more movies were filmed in color after the end of WWII, as the industry in America came to view color an essential to attracting audiences in its competition with television, which remained a black-and-white medium until the mid-60s. By the end of the 1960s, color had become the norm for film makers, and by the 1980s, an expectation of the younger generations by then comprising the majority of the audience for commercial films. Only in rare exceptions is black-and-white film now used; the choice is motivated by artistic reasons.

Motion Picture Industry

The making and showing of motion pictures became a source of profit almost as soon the process was invented. Upon seeing how successful their new invention, and its product, was in their native France, the Lumieres quickly set about touring the Continent to exhibit the first films privately to royalty and publicly to the masses. In each country, they would normally add new, local scenes to their catalogue and, quickly enough, found local entrepreneurs in the various countries of Europe to buy their equipment and photograph, export, import and screen additional product commercially. The Oberammergau Passion play of 1898 was the first commercial motion picture ever produced. Other pictures soon followed, and motion pictures became a separate industry that overshadowed the vaudeville world. Dedicated theaters and companies formed specifically to produce and distribute films, while motion picture actors became major celebrities and commanded huge fees for their performances. Already by 1917, Charlie Chaplin had a contract that called for an annual salary of one million dollars.

In the United States today, much of the film industry is centered around Hollywood. Other regional centers exist in many parts of the world, and the Indian film industry annually produces the largest number of films in the world. Though the expense involved in making movies has led cinema production to concentrate under the auspices of movie studios, recent advances in affordable film making equipment have allowed independent film productions to flourish.

Profit is a key force in the industry, due to the costly nature of filmmaking; yet many filmmakers strive to create works of lasting social significance. The Academy Awards are the most prominent film awards in the United States, providing recognition each year to films, ostensibly based on their artistic merits. Also, film quickly came to be used in education, in lieu of or in addition to lectures and texts.

When it is initially produced, a film is normally shown to audiences in a movie theater. The first theater designed exclusively for cinema opened in Pittsburgh, Pennsylvania in 1905. Thousands of such theaters were built or converted from existing facilities within a few years. In the United States, these theaters came to be known as nickelodeons, because admission typically cost a nickel (5 cents).

Typically, one film is the featured presentation. A feature film is sometimes defined as any film more than 60 minutes in length (90-120 minutes is typical, and a few films run up to 4 hours or more). Before showing this film, the theater may have shorter presentations. In Europe there has been advertising since before WWII; it has appeared in American cinemas in the late twentieth century. Historically, the feature presentation was often preceded by newsreels and short films, especially animation. There were "double features"; typically, a high quality "A picture" rented by an independent theater for a lump sum, and a "B picture" of lower quality rented for a percentage of the gross receipts. Today, the bulk of the material shown before the feature film (those in theaters) consists of previews for upcoming movies (also known as trailers).

Originally, all films are made to be shown in movie theaters. The development of television has allowed films to be broadcast to larger audiences, usually after the film is no longer being shown in theaters. Recording technology has also enabled consumers to rent or buy copies of films on video tape or DVD, and Internet downloads may be available and have started to become revenue sources for the film companies. Some films are now made specifically for these other venues, being released as made-for-TV movies or direct-to-video movies. These are often considered to be of inferior quality compared to theatrical releases. And indeed, some films that are rejected by their own studios upon completion are dumped into these markets.

The movie theater pays an average of about 55% of its ticket sales to the movie studio, as film rental fees. The actual percentage starts with a number higher than that, and decreases as the duration of a film's showing continues, as an incentive to theaters to keep movies in the theater longer. However, today's barrage of highly marketed movies ensures that most movies are shown in first-run theaters for less than 8 weeks. There are a few movies every year that defy this rule, often limited-release movies that start in only a few theaters and actually grow their theater count through good word-of-mouth and reviews.

Development of Film Technology

Filmstock consists of a transparent celluloid, polyester, or other plastic base coated with an emulsion containing light-sensitive chemicals. Cellulose nitrate was the first type of film base used to record motion pictures, but due to its flammability was eventually replaced by safer materials. Stock widths and the film format for images on the reel have had a rich history, though most large commercial films are still shot on (and distributed to theaters) as 35 mm prints.

Originally moving picture film was shot at various speeds using hand-cranked cameras; then the speed for mechanized cameras and projectors was standardized at 16 frames per second, which was faster than much existing hand-cranked footage. A new standard speed, 24 frames per second, came with the introduction of sound. Improvements since the late 1800s include the mechanization of cameras, allowing them to record at a consistent speed, the invention of more sophisticated filmstocks and lenses, allowing directors to film in increasingly dim conditions, and the development of synchronized sound, allowing sound to be recorded at exactly the same speed as its corresponding action. The soundtrack can be recorded separately from shooting the film, but for live-action pictures many parts of the soundtrack are usually recorded simultaneously.

As a medium, film is not limited to motion pictures, since the technology developed as the basis for photography. It can be used to present a progressive sequence of still images in the form of a slideshow. Film has also been incorporated into multimedia presentations, and often has importance as primary historical documentation. However, historic films have problems in terms of preservation and storage, and the motion picture industry is exploring many alternatives. Most movies on cellulose nitrate base have been copied onto modern safety films. Some studios save three B&W negatives exposed through red, green, and blue filters. Digital methods have also been used to restore and preserve films. Film preservation of decaying film stock is a matter of concern to both film historians and archivists, and to companies interested in preserving their existing products in order to make them available to future generations.

Some films in recent decades have been recorded using analog video technology similar to that used in television production. Modern digital video cameras and digital projectors are gaining ground as well. These approaches are extremely beneficial to moviemakers, especially because footage can be evaluated and edited without waiting for the film stock to be processed. Yet the migration is gradual, and as of 2005 most major motion pictures are still recorded on film.

TELEVISION

Television is a telecommunication system for broadcasting and receiving moving pictures and sound over a distance. The term has come to refer to all the aspects of television programming and transmission as well. The word television is a hybrid word, coming from both Greek and Latin. "Tele-" is Greek for "far", while "-vision" is from the Latin "visio", meaning "vision" or "sight". It is often abbreviated as TV. The development of television technology can be partitioned along two lines: those developments that depended upon both mechanical and electronic principles, and those which are purely electronic. From the latter descended all modern televisions, but these would not have been possible without discoveries and insights from the mechanical systems.

Electromechanical Television

The German student Paul Gottlieb Nipkow proposed and patented the first electromechanical television system in 1885. Nipkow's spinning disk design is credited with being the first television image rasterizer, however, it wasn't until 1907 that developments in amplification tube technology made the design practical. Meanwhile, Constantin Perskyi had coined the word television in a paper read to the International Electricity Congress at the International World Fair in Paris on August 25, 1900. Perskeyi's paper reviewed the existing electromechanical technologies, mentioning the work of Nipkow and others.

From 1907 to 1910, Boris Rosing and his student Vladimir Zworykin demonstrated a television system that used a mechanical mirror-drum scanner in the transmitter and the electronic Braun tube (cathode ray tube) in the receiver. Rosing disappeared during the Bolshevik revolution of 1917, but Zworykin later went to work for RCA to build a purely electronic television, the design of which was eventually found to violate patents by Philo Taylor Farnsworth.

A mechanically-scanned analogue television system was first demonstrated in London in February 1924 by John Logie Baird with an image of Felix the Cat and a moving picture by Baird on October 30, 1925. In 1928 Baird's company broadcast the first transatlantic Television signal, between London and New York, and the first shore to ship transmission. He also demonstrated an electromechanical colour, infrare and stereoscopic television, using additional lenses, disks and filters. In parallel he developed a video disk recording system dubbed "Phonovision"; a number of the Phonovision[1] recordings, dating back to 1927, still exist. In 1929 he became involved in the first experimental electromechanical television service in Germany. In 1931 he made the first live transmission, of the Epsom Derby. In 1932 he demonstrated ultra-short wave television. Baird's system was tested by the BBC, who later discontinued its use in 1937 in favor of purely electronic television.

Electronic Television

Although the discoveries of Nipkow, Rosing, Baird and others were extraordinary, little of their technology is used in modern television. By 1934, all electromechanical television systems were outmoded. A.A. Campbell-Swinton wrote a letter to Nature on the 18 June 1908 describing his concept of electronic television using the cathode ray tube, which had been invented in 1897 by the German physicist and Nobel prize winner Karl Ferdinand Braun. He proposed using an electron beam in both the camera and the receiver, which could be steered electronically to produce moving pictures. He lectured on the subject in 1911 and displayed circuit diagrams, but no one, including Swinton, knew how to realize the design. Even though his system was never built, the cathode ray tube is still used in almost all television sets to display images until today.

A fully electronic system was first demonstrated by Philo Taylor Farnsworth in the autumn of 1927. Farnsworth, a Mormon farm boy from Rigby, Idaho, first envisioned his system at age 14. He discussed the idea with his high school chemistry teacher, who could think of no reason why it would not work. He continued to pursue the idea at Brigham Young Academy. At age 21, he demonstrated a working system at his own laboratory in San Francisco. His breakthrough freed television from reliance on spinning discs and other mechanical parts. All modern picture tube televisions descend directly from his design.

Vladimir Zworykin is also sometimes cited as the father of electronic television because of his invention of the iconoscope in 1923 and his invention of the kinescope in 1929. His design was one of the first to demonstrate a television system with all the features of modern picture tubes. His previous work with Rosing on electromechanical television gave him key insights into how to produce such a system, but his (and RCA's) claim to being its original inventor was largely invalidated by three facts: a) Zworykin's 1923 patent presented an incomplete design, incapable of working in its given form (it was not until 1933 that Zworykin achieved a working implementation), b) the 1923 patent application was not granted until 1938, and not until it had been seriously revised, and c) courts eventually found that RCA was in violation of the television design patented by Philo Taylor Farnsworth, whose lab Zworykin had visited while working on his designs for RCA.

The controversy over whether it was first Farnsworth or Zworykin who invented modern television is still hotly debated today. Some of this debate stems from the fact that while Farnsworth appears to have gotten there first, it was RCA that first marketed working television sets, and it was RCA employees who first wrote the history of television. Even though Farnsworth eventually won the legal battle over this issue, he was never able to fully capitalize financially on his invention.

Broadcast Television

Television antenna on a rooftopThe first long distance public television broadcast was from Washington, DC to New York City and occurred on April 7, 1927. The image shown was of then Commerce Secretary Herbert Hoover. The first analogue service was WGY, Schenectady, New York inaugurated on May 11, 1928. The first British Television Play, "The Man with the Flower in his Mouth", was transmitted in July 1930. CBS's New York City station began broadcasting the first regular seven days a week television schedule in the U. S. on July 21, 1931. The first broadcast included Mayor James J. Walker, Kate Smith, and George Gershwin. The first all-electronic television service was started in Los Angeles, CA by Don Lee Broadcasting. Their start date was December 23, 1931 on W6XAO - later KTSL. Originally, mechanical equipment was used, but in June of 1936 a 300-line all-electronic service was started.

In Germany, regular service started on March 22, 1935, and one year later, the Berlin Summer Olympic Games were televised to places in Berlin and Hamburg.

In 1932 the BBC launched a service using Baird's 30-line system and these transmissions continued until 11 September 1935. On November 2, 1936 the BBC began broadcasting a dual-system service, alternating on a weekly basis between Marconi-EMI's high-resolution (405 lines per picture) service and Baird's improved 240-line standard from Alexandra Palace in London. Six months later, the corporation decided that Marconi-EMI's electronic picture gave the superior picture, and adopted that as their standard. This service is described as "the world's first regular high-definition public television service", since a regular television service had been broadcast earlier on a 180-line standard in Germany. The outbreak of the Second World War caused the service to be suspended. TV transmissions only resumed from Alexandra Palace in 1946.

The first live transcontinental television broadcast took place in San Francisco, California from the Japanese Peace Treaty Conference on September 4, 1951. In 1958, the CBC completed the longest television network in the world, from Sydney, Nova Scotia to Victoria, British Columbia. Reportedly, the first continuous live broadcast of a breaking news story in the world was conducted by the CBC during the Springhill Mining Disaster which began on October 23 of that year.

Programming is broadcast on television stations. At first, terrestrial broadcasting was the only way television could be distributed. Because bandwidth was limited, government regulation was normal. In the US, the Federal Communications Commission allowed stations to broadcast advertisements, but insisted on public service programming commitments as a requirement for a license. By contrast, the United Kingdom chose a different route, imposing a television licence fee on owners of television reception equipment, to fund the BBC, which had public service as part of its Royal Charter. Development of cable and satellite means of distribution in the 1970s pushed businessmen to target channels towards a certain audience, and enabled the rise of subscription-based television channels, such as HBO and Sky. Practically every country in the world now has developed at least one television channel. Television has grown up all over the world, enabling every country to share aspects of their culture and society with others.

By the late 1980s, 98% of all homes in the U.S. had at least one TV set. On average, Americans watch four hours of television per day. An estimated two-thirds of Americans got most of their news about the world from TV, and nearly half got all of their news from TV. These figures are now estimated to be significantly higher.

Color Television

Güillermo González Camarena, invented the first color TX and first TV XEG. He holds the design and patent to color television systems from 1940, 1942, 1960 and 1962. In August 31, 1946 he sent his first color transmission from his lab in the offices of The Mexican League of Radio Experiments in Lucerna St. #1, in Mexico City. The video signal was transmited in 115 MHz. and the audio in a band of 40 meters. RCA claims they did it in 1946 but Camarena's patent has an earlier month. Also, there are previous attempts or designs but none worked properly. Camarena's was the first successful one.

TV Sets

The earliest television sets were radios with the addition of a television device consisting of a neon tube with a mechanically spinning disk that produced a red postage-stamp size image . The first publicly broadcast electronic service was in Germany in March 1935. It had 180 lines of resolution and was only available in 22 public viewing rooms. One of the first major broadcasts involved the 1936 Berlin Olympics. The Germans had a 441-line system in the autumn of 1937. An example of an early television set is called a rotary dial-tune TV is outdated technology for a television set. This is one of the earliest technologies for TV turners. When the quartz-synthesized turners for TVs came out, rotary dial-tune turner technology was gradually obsoleting.

Television usage skyrocketed after World War II with war-related technological advances and additional disposable income. Prior to the war, in the 1930s, TV receivers cost the equivalent of US$7000 in 2001, and had little available programming. Rotary dial-tune TVs were the earliest method of channel tuning until it became obsolete in the 90's.

For many years different countries used different technical standards. France initially adopted the German 441-line standard but later upgraded to 819 lines, which gave the highest picture definition of any analogue TV system, approximately four times the resolution of the British 405-line system. Eventually the whole of Europe switched to the 625-line standard, once more following Germany's example. Meanwhile in North America the original 525-line standard was retained.

A television with a VHF "rabbit ears" antenna and a loop UHF antenna.Television in its original and still most popular form involves sending images and sound over radio waves in the VHF and UHF bands, which are received by a receiver (a television set). In this sense, it is an extension of radio. Broadcast television requires an antenna (aerial). This can be an external antenna mounted outside or smaller antennas mounted on or near the television. Typically this is an adjustable dipole antenna called "rabbit ears" for the VHF band and a small loop antenna for the UHF band.

Some early television sets, especially British ones, contained valves and other pre-solid state electronic components which generated a considerable amount of heat even when the set was switched off. As a result, up until at least the mid-1970s, television stations would air announcements reminding viewers to unplug their sets before going to bed for the night, since the heat build-up in the back of the set was a considerable fire hazard.

Color television became available in the U.S. on December 30 of 1953, backed by the Columbia Broadcasting System (CBS) network. The government approved the color broadcast system proposed by CBS, but when RCA came up with a subcarrier system that made it possible to view color broadcasts in black and white on unmodified old black and white TV sets, CBS dropped their own proposal and used the new one.

The first publicly announced experimental TV broadcast of a program using RCA's "compatible color" system was an episode of Kukla, Fran and Ollie on August 30, 1953. NBC was the first network to have a regularly scheduled color program on the air . The networks slowly reformed into the color standard, and all three broadcast networks were airing full color schedules by the 1966-67 broadcast season.

European color television was developed somewhat later and was hindered by a continuing division on technical standards. Having decided to adopt a higher-definition 625-line system for monochrome transmissions, with a lower frame rate but with a higher overall bandwidth, Europeans could not directly adopt the US color standard, which was widely perceived as wanting anyway, because of its tint control problems. There was no urgency either, since there were still few sets overall and no commercial motivations, European television broadcasters being state-owned at the time.

As a consequence, although work on various color encoding systems started already in the 1950s, with the first SECAM patent being registered in 1956, many years had passed till the first broadcasts actually started in 1967. Unsatisfied with the performance of NTSC and of initial SECAM implementations, the Germans decided to create PAL (phase alternating line) at the beginning of the 1960s, staying closer to NTSC but borrowing some ideas from SECAM. The French continued with SECAM, notably involving Russians in the development.

The first color broadcast in Europe was by BBC2 in the UK in the summer of 1967, using PAL. Germans did their first broadcast in September (PAL), while the French in October (SECAM). PAL was eventually adopted by West Germany, the UK, Australia, New Zealand, much of Africa, Asia and South America, and most Western European countries except France.

Apart for France and Luxembourg, SECAM was adopted by Soviet Union, much of Eastern Europe, much of Africa and of the Middle East. Both systems broadcast on UHF frequencies, the VHF being used for legacy black & white, 405 lines in UK or 819 lines in France, till the beginning of the eighties!

Starting in the 1990s, modern television sets diverged into three different trends:

— standalone TV sets;

— integrated systems with DVD players and/or VHS VCR capabilities built into the TV set itself;

— component systems with separate big-screen video monitor, tuner, audio system which the owner connects the pieces together as a high-end home theater system. This approach appeals to videophiles who prefer components that can be upgraded separately.

There are many kinds of video monitors used in modern TV sets. The most common are direct view CRTs for up to 40 inch or 100 cm (in 4:3) and 46 inch or 115 cm (in 16:9) diagonally; most big screen TVs (up to over 100 inch (254 cm)) use projection technology. Three types of projection systems are used in projection TVs: CRT-based, LCD-based, and DLP(reflective micromirror chip)-based.

Modern advances have brought flat screens to TV that use active matrix LCD or plasma display technology. Flat panel LCDs and plasma displays are as little as 4 inch or 10 cm thick and can be hung on a wall like a picture or put over a pedestal. They are multifunctional, because they are used like computer monitors too. Nowadays some TVs integrates a pair of ports to connect computer cases and peripherals to it or to connect the set to an A/V home network (HAVI).

9

Internet as a Global Medium of Communication

During the last decade of the 20th century, the advent of the World Wide Web marked the first era in which any individual could have a means of exposure on the scale of mass media. For the first time, anyone with a web site can address a global audience, although serving high levels of web traffic is still expensive. It is possible that the rise of peer-to-peer technologies may have begun the process of making the cost of bandwidth manageable.

The computer as a new communication technology opens a space for scholars to rethink assumptions and categories, and perhaps even to find new insights into traditional communication technologies. The Internet has become impossible to ignore. Even people who do not own a computer and have no opportunity to "surf the net" could not have missed the news stories about the Internet, many of which speculate about its effects on the ever-increasing number of people who are on line. Until recently, mass communications researchers have overlooked not only the Internet but the entire field of computer-mediated communication, staying instead with the traditional forms of broadcast and print media that fit much more conveniently into models for appropriate research topics and theories of mass communication.

If mass communications researchers continue to largely disregard the research potential of the Internet, their theories about communication will become less useful. Not only will the discipline be left behind, it will also miss an opportunity to explore and rethink answers to some of the central questions of mass communications research, questions that go to the heart of the model of source-message-receiver with which the field has struggled.

Mass media researchers have traditionally organized themselves around a specific communications medium. The newspaper, for instance, is a more precisely defined area of interest than printing-press-mediated communication, which embraces more specialized areas, such as company brochures or wedding invitations. Of course, there is far more than a semantic difference between conceptualizing a new communication technology by its communicative form than by the technology itself. The tradition of mass communication research has accepted newspapers, radio, and television as its objects of study for social, political, and economic reasons. As technology changes and media converge, those research categories must become flexible. Mass communications researchers have overlooked the potential of the Internet for several reasons. The Internet was developed in bits and pieces by hobbyists, students, and academics. It didn't fit researchers' ideas about mass media, locked, as they have been, into models of print and broadcast media.

Computer-mediated communication (CMC) at first resembled interpersonal communication and was relegated to the domain of other fields, such as education, management information science, and library science. These fields, in fact, have been doing research into CMC for nearly 20 years, and many of their ideas about CMC have proven useful in looking at the phenomenon as a mass medium. Both education and business researchers have seen the computer as a technology through which communication was mediated, and both lines of research have been concerned with the effects of this new medium.

Disciplinary lines have long kept researchers from seeing the whole picture of the communication process. Cathcart and Gumpert recognized this problem when they noted how speech communication definitions "have minimized the role of media and channel in the communication process", even as mass communication definitions disregarded the ways media function in interpersonal communication: "We are quite convinced that the traditional division of communication study into interpersonal, group and public, and mass communication is inadequate because it ignores the pervasiveness of media".

The major constraint on doing mass communication research into the Internet, however, has been theoretical. In searching for theories to apply to group software systems, researchers in MIS have recognized that communication studies needed new theoretical models: "The emergence of new technologies such as GSS (Group Support Systems, software that allows group decision-making), which combine aspects of both interpersonal interaction and mass media, presents something of a challenge to communication theory. With new technologies, the line between the various contexts begins to blur, and it is unclear that models based on mass media or face-to-face contexts are adequate".

Not only have theoretical models constrained research, but the most basic assumptions behind researchers' theories of mass media effects have kept them from being able to see the Internet as a new mass medium. DeFleur and Ball-Rokeach's attitude toward computers in the fifth edition of their Theories of Mass Communication is typical. They compare computers to telephones, dismissing the idea of computer communication as mass communication: "Even if computer literacy were to become universal, and even if every household had a personal computer equipped with a modem, it is difficult to see how a new system of mass communication could develop from this base alone".

The fact that DeFleur and Ball-Rokeach find it difficult to envision this development may well be a result of their own constrained perspective. Taking the telephone analogy a step further, Lana Rakow points out that the lack of research on the telephone was due in part to researchers' inability to see it as a mass medium. The telephone also became linked to women, who embraced the medium as a way to overcome social isolation.

However, a new communication technology can throw the facades of the old into sharp relief. Marshall McLuhan recognized this when, speaking of the computer, he wrote, "The advent of a new medium often reveals the lineaments and assumptions, as it were, of an old medium" . In effect, a new communication technology may perform an almost postmodern function of making the unpresentable perceptible, as Lyotard might put it. In creating new configurations of sources, messages, and receivers, new communication technologies force researchers to examine their old definitions. What is a mass audience? What is a communication medium? How are messages mediated?

Daniel Bell recognized the slippery nature of the term mass society and how its many definitions lacked a sense of reality: "What strikes one about these varied uses of the concept of mass society is how little they reflect or relate to the complex, richly striated social relations of the real world". Similarly, the term mass media, with its roots in ideas of mass society, has always been difficult to define. There is much at stake in hanging on to traditional definitions of mass media, as shown in the considerable anxiety in recent years over the loss of the mass audience and its implications for the liberal pluralist state.

The convergence of communication technologies, as represented by the computer, has set off this fear of demassification, as audiences become more and more fragmented. Critical researchers have long questioned the assumptions implicit in traditional media effects definitions, looking instead to the social, economic, and historical contexts that gave rise to institutional conceptions of media. Such analysis, Fejes notes, can lead to another unquestioning set of assumptions about the media's ability to affect audiences. As Ang has pointed out, abandoning the idea of the mass media and their audiences impedes an investigation of media institutions' power to create messages that are consumed by real people. If the category of mass medium becomes too fuzzy to define, traditional effects researchers will be left without dependent variables, and critical scholars will have no means of discussing issues of social and political power.

A new communication technology such as the Internet allows scholars to rethink, rather than abandon, definitions and categories. When the Internet is conceptualized as a mass medium, what becomes clear is that neither mass nor medium can be precisely defined for all situations, but instead must be continually rearticulated depending on the situation.

The Internet is a multifaceted mass medium, that is, it contains many different configurations of communication. Its varied forms show the connection between interpersonal and mass communication that has been an object of study since the two-step flow associated the two. Chaffee and Mutz have called for an exploration of this relationship that begins "with a theory that spells out what effects are of interest, and what aspects of communication might produce them. The Internet offers a chance to develop and to refine that theory.

The Internet plays with the source-message-receiver features of the traditional mass communication model, sometimes putting them into traditional patterns, sometimes putting them into entirely new configurations. Internet communication takes many forms, from World Wide Web pages operated by major news organizations to Usenet groups discussing folk music to E-mail messages among colleagues and friends.

The Internet's communication forms can be understood as a continuum. Each point in the traditional model of the communication process can, in fact, vary from one to a few to many on the Internet. Sources of the messages can range from one person in E-mail communication, to a social group in a Listserv or Usenet group, to a group of professional journalists in a World Wide Web page.

The messages themselves can be traditional journalistic news stories created by a reporter and editor, stories created over a long period of time by many people, or simply conversations, such as in an Internet Relay Chat group. The receivers, or audiences, of these messages can also number from one to potentially millions, and may or may not move fluidly from their role as audience members to producers of messages.

Producers and audiences on the Internet can be grouped generally into four categories:

(a) one-to-one asynchronous communication, such as E-mail;

(b) many-to-many asynchronous communication, such as Usenet, electronic bulletin boards, and Listservers that require the receiver to sign up for a service or log on to a program to access messages around a particular topic or topics;

(c) synchronous communication that can be one-to-one, one-to-few, or one-to-many and can be organized around a topic, the construction of an object, or role playing, such as MUDs (Multi-User Dungeons and their various transformations as MOOs, MUCKs and MUSHs), Internet Relay Chat and chat rooms on commercial services; and

(d) asynchronous communication generally characterized by the receiver's need to seek out the site in order to access information, which may involve many-to-one, one-to-one, or one-to-many source-receiver relationships (e.g., Web sites, gophers, and FTP sites).

Reconceptualizing the audience for the communication that takes place on the Internet is a major problem, one that becomes increasingly important as commercial information providers enter the Internet in greater numbers. To date, thousands of commercial sources have created home pages or gopher sites for people to access their services or information about those services.

As of September 1995, search tools on the Internet turned up as many as 123 different U.S. newspaper services and more than 1,300 magazine services with distinct web sites. Some newspapers seem to be creating home pages to mark their place in cyberspace until their managers determine how to make them commercially viable. Others may be moving to the Internet out of fear of the electronic competition. Thus, it remains difficult to envision the future of traditional mass media on the Internet-who will be the audience, how will that audience access the information and entertainment services, and what profit might be made from the services?

A parallel question investigates the impact of Internet communication on the audience. Mass communications researchers will want to examine information-seeking and knowledge gaps as well as a range of uses-and-gratifications-based questions concerning the audience. Since the Internet is also being used for entertainment as well as information, effects researchers will want to know whether the Internet is a functional equivalent of other entertainment media and whether there are negative effects in the distribution of pornography and verbal attacks on members of the audience. There are also questions of audience addiction to certain types of Internet communication and entertainment.

When the uses of the Internet as a mass medium are explored, questions arise about the nature of its communicative content. As commercial providers increase on the Internet, and more political information is provided, the problem of who sets the agenda for the new medium also becomes a concern.

Credibility is another issue with mass media. Traditional mass media make certain claims about the veracity of their information. The Internet makes few such claims at the moment, and it is possible that the concept of credibility will also change as a result. Recently, on a feminist newsnet group, an individual began to post what appeared to be off-base comments to a serious discussion of feminist issues. Several days later it was determined that "Mike" was a computer-generated personage and not a real contributor to the discussion at all. At present there is no way to know when the Mikes on the Internet are even real, let alone credible. Consequently, we wish to underscore the fundamental importance of this issue.

Traditional mass media have addressed the issue within their organizations, hiring editors and fact checkers to determine what information is accurate. Source credibility will vary on the Internet, with commercial media sites carrying relatively more credibility and unknown sources carrying less. A much greater burden will be placed on the user to determine how much faith to place in any given source.

Another question relates to the interchangeability of producers and receivers of content. One of the Internet's most widely touted advantages is that an audience member may also be a message producer. To what extent is that really the case? We may discover a fair amount about the producers of messages from the content of their electronic messages, but what about the lurkers? Who are they and how big is this group? To what extent do lurkers resemble the more passive audience of television sitcoms? And why do they remain lurkers and not also become information providers? Is there something about the nature of the medium that prevents their participation?

Other questions concern production of culture, social control, and political communication. Will the Internet ultimately be accessible to all? How are groups excluded from participation? Computers were originally created to wage war and have been developed in an extremely specific, exclusive culture. Can we trace those cultural influences in the way messages are produced on the Internet?

Mass Communication Theories and Internet

In an overview of research on computers in education, O'Shea and Self note that the learner-as-bucket theory had dominated. In this view, knowledge is like a liquid that is poured into the student, a metaphor similar to mass communication's magic-bullet theory. This brings up another aspect to consider in looking at mass communication research into CMC-the applicability of established theories and methodologies to the new medium. As new communication technologies are developed, researchers seem to use the patterns of research established for existing technologies to explain the uses and effects of the new media. Research in group communication, for example, has been used to examine the group uses of E-mail networks. Researchers have studied concepts of status, decision-making quality, social presence, social control, and group norms as they have been affected by a technology that permitted certain changes in group communication.

This kind of transfer of research patterns from one communication technology to another is not unusual. Wartella and Reeves studied the history of American mass communication research in the area of children and the media. With each new medium, the effects of content on children were discussed as a social problem in public debate. As Wartella and Reeves note, researchers responded to the public controversy over the adoption of a new media technology in American life.

In approaching the study of the Internet as a mass medium, the following established concepts seem to be useful starting points. Some of these have originated in the study of interpersonal or small group communication; others have been used to examine mass media. Some relate to the nature of the medium, while others focus on the audience for the medium.

Critical Mass

This conceptual framework has been adopted from economists, physicists, and sociologists by organizational communication and diffusion of innovation scholars to better understand the size of the audience needed for a new technology to be considered successful and the nature of collective action as applied to electronic media use.

For any medium to be considered a mass medium, and therefore economically viable to advertisers, a critical mass of adopters must be achieved. Interactive media only become useful as more and more people adopt, or as Rogers states, "the usefulness of a new communication system increases for all adopters with each additional adopter" Initially, the critical mass notion works against adoption, since it takes a number of other users to be seen as advantageous to adopt. For example, the telephone or an E-mail system was not particularly useful to the first adopters because most people were unable to receive their messages or converse with them.

Valente notes that the critical mass is achieved when about 10 to 20 percent of the population has adopted the innovation. When this level has been reached, the innovation can be spread to the rest of the social system. Adoption of computers in U.S. households has well surpassed this figure, but the modem connections needed for Internet connection lag somewhat behind.

Because a collection of communication services-electronic bulletin boards, Usenet groups, E-mail, Internet Relay Chats, home pages, gophers, and so forth-comprise the Internet, the concept of critical mass on the Internet could be looked upon as a variable, rather than a fixed percentage of adopters. Fewer people are required for sustaining an Internet Relay Chat conference or a Multi-User Dungeon than may be required for an electronic bulletin board or another type of discussion group.

A relatively large number of E-mail users are required for any two people to engage in conversation, yet only those two people constitute the critical mass for any given conversation. For a bulletin board to be viable, its content must have depth and variety. If the audience who also serve as the source of information for the BBS is too small, the bulletin board cannot survive for lack of content. A much larger *critical mass* will be needed for such a group to maintain itself-perhaps as many as 100 or more. The discretionary data base, as defined by Connolly and Thorn is a "shared pool of data to which several participants may, if they choose, separately contribute information". If no one contributes, the data base cannot exist. It requires a critical mass of participants to carry the free riders in the system, thus supplying this public good to all members, participants, or free riders. Though applied to organizations, this refinement of the critical mass theory is a useful way of thinking about Listservs, electronic bulletin boards, Usenet groups, and other Internet services, where participants must hold up their end of the process through written contributions. Each of these specific Internet services can be viewed as we do specific television stations, small town newspapers, or special interest magazines. None of these may reach a strictly mass audience, but in conjunction with all the other stations, newspapers, and magazines distributed in the country, they constitute mass media categories. So the Internet itself would be considered the mass medium, while the individual sites and services are the components of which this medium is comprised.

Interactivity

This concept has been assumed to be a natural attribute of interpersonal communication, but, as explicated by Rafaeli, it is more recently applied to all new media, from two-way cable to the Internet. From Rafaeli's perspective, the most useful basis of inquiry for interactivity would be one grounded in responsiveness. Rafaeli's definition of interactivity "recognizes three pertinent levels: two-way (noninteractive) communication, reactive (or quasi-interactive) communication, and fully interactive communication".

Anyone working to conceptualize Internet communication would do well to draw on this variable and follow Rafaeli's lead when he notes that the value of a focus on interactivity is that the concept cuts across the mass versus interpersonal distinctions usually made in the fields of inquiry. It.is also helpful to consider interactivity to be variable in nature, increasing or decreasing with the particular Internet service in question.

Uses and Gratifications

Though research of mass media use from a uses-and-gratifications perspective has not been prevalent in the communication literature in recent years, it may help provide a useful framework from which to begin the work on Internet communication. Both Walther and Rafaeli concur in this conclusion. The logic of the uses-and-gratifications approach, based in functional analysis, is derived from "(1) the social and psychological origins of (2) needs, which generate (3) expectations of (4) the mass media and other sources, which lead to (5) differential patterns of media exposure (or engagement in other activities), resulting in (7) other consequences, perhaps mostly unintended ones."

Rosengren modified the original approach in one way by noting that the "needs" in the original model had to be perceived as problems and some potential solution to those problems needed to be perceived by the audience. Rafaeli regards the move away from effects research to a uses-and-gratifications approach as essential to the study of electronic bulletin boards. He is predisposed to examine electronic bulletin boards in the context of play or Ludenic theory, an extension of the uses-and-gratifications approach, which is clearly a purpose that drives much of Internet use by a wide spectrum of the population. Rafaeli summarizes the importance of this paradigm for electronic communication by noting uses-and-gratifications' comprehensive nature in a media environment where computers have not only home and business applications, but also work and play functions.

Additionally, the uses-and-gratifications approach presupposes a degree of audience activity, whether instrumental or ritualized. The concept of audience activity should be included in the study of Internet communication, and it already has been incorporated in one examination of the Cleveland Freenet.

Media Richness Theory

These approaches have been applied to CMC use by organizational communication researchers to account for interpersonal effects. But social presence theory stems from an attempt to determine the differential properties of various communication media, including mass media, in the degree of social cues inherent in the technology. In general, CMC, with its lack of visual and other nonverbal cues, is said to be extremely low in social presence in comparison to face-to-face communication.

Media richness theory differentiates between lean and rich media by the bandwidth or number of cue systems within each medium. This approach suggests that because CMC is a lean channel, it is useful for simple or unequivocal messages, and also that it is more efficient "because shadow functions and coordinated interaction efforts are unnecessary. For receivers to understand clearly more equivocal information, information that is ambiguous, emphatic, or emotional, however, a richer medium should be used".

Unfortunately, much of the research on media richness and social presence has been one-shot experiments or field studies. Given the ambiguous results of such studies in business and education, it can be expected that over a longer time period, people who communicate on Usenets and bulletin boards will restore some of those social cues and thus make the medium richer than its technological parameters would lead us to expect. As Walther argues: "It appears that the conclusion that CMC is less socioemotional or personal than face-to-face communication is based on incomplete measurement of the latter form, and it may not be true whatsoever, even in restricted laboratory settings". Further, he notes that though researchers recognize that nonverbal social context cues convey formality and status inequality, "they have reached their conclusion about CMC/face-to-face differences without actually observing the very non-verbal cues through which these effects are most likely to be performed".

Clearly, there is room for more work on the social presence and media richness of Internet communication. It could turn out that the Internet contains a very high degree of media richness relative to other mass media, to which it has insufficiently been compared and studied. Ideas about social presence also tend to disguise the subtle kinds of social control that goes on on the Net through language, such as flaming.

Network Approaches

Grant has suggested that researchers approach new communication technologies through network analysis, to better address the issues of social influence and critical mass. Conceptualizing Internet communities as networks might be a very useful approach. As discussed earlier, old concepts of senders and receivers are inappropriate to the study of the Internet. Studying the network of users of any given Internet service can incorporate the concept of interactivity and the interchangeability of message producers and receivers. The computer allows a more efficient analysis of network communication, but researchers will need to address the ethical issues related to studying people's communication without their permission.

These are just a few of the core concepts and theoretical frameworks that should be applied to a mass communication perspective on Internet communication. Reconceptualizing the Internet from this perspective will allow researchers both to continue to use the structures of traditional media studies and to develop new ways of thinking about those structures. It is, finally, a question of taxonomy. Thomas Kuhn has noted the ways in which similarity and resemblance are important in creating scientific paradigms. As Kuhn points out, scientists facing something new "can often agree on the particular symbolic expression appropriate to it, even though none of them has seen that particular expression before" .

Internet and Modern Consumers

Today we witness a complete change in the nature of mass communication, the ripples expand from millions of points. Some of these ripples fade, dispersing as minor vibrations. Others, however, coincident in direction, raise implications like a breaking Tsunami. Until very recently, the consumer of information relied mostly on mass media, as opposed to interactive means. It is not called mass media because it is directed towards the "simple masses" like one might think of the tabloid press. It's name, mass, refers to a format based on mass consumption.

Information travels one way, packaged like any other Twinkie, formatted uniformly regardless of the user. In this sense, a classic novel is no different than a periodical or daily paper. That's old news, so to speak, but now it's getting truly engaging. We are at a span in literary history where mass media is falling to the worldwide interactive flow of information. The tide is finally coming in on a regular basis, and some sandcastles are about to fall.

Mass Media, by its nature, allows its producers to comment without questions and state as fact without support. The consumer may protest by refusing to buy that publication. The consumer may disagree, add to, or question further in the form of a letter to the editor. If the format encourages a controlled dialogue, and the editor chooses to publish that letter, the individual may see public satisfaction within a couple months. Even so, very rarely does a reader's letter elicit the same attention as a featured article. In the end, though, control lies with the producer of the publication, as does the last word. It is, after all, their product. Traditionally, because individuals knowledgeable, or even interested in a topic were difficult to locate, to find differing opinions from other sources, one had to search it out. One could either invest time at the library, money at the bookstore, or hope to come across a special on public television.

If someone desired to impart his/her own information to the same audience, they would have to publish themselves or find someone willing to publish their ideas, work to distribute that publication, and somehow promote it so that others would read it. It costs a lot of money, and takes a lot of time. Publishing in print in order to raise your voice to a specific audience is not conducive to a free exchange of ideas. In publications that claim to make unbiased and educated reviews of equipment which might constitute a substantial economical investment, this has serious implications.

Reviewers and editors of audio and video publications carry an assumed authority as experts. They do, to be fair, have more experience with a variety of equipment than the average enthusiast does. Particular magazines will vary in practice, but the position established by the nature of mass media provides an extreme potential for abuse. Scholarly journals and trade magazines do have a great deal of peer review, but writers for publications intended for the "average" consumer may assert speculation or hearsay as technical fact without fear of embarrassing rebuttal.

Individuals without the least amount of understanding, let alone training, can comment on the workings of the latest, or even the most conventional technology wearing a guise of authority, with only their editor to answer to. In some cases, the editor, technical or not, may not be qualified to make decisions about what is truthful and responsible to print, yet still not defer the decision to someone better suited. Some editors might even be extremely qualified, but also have an agenda as it relates to advertisers.

Although many very good publications address subjective and objective issues, others may spread false rumors, or utter misinformation with what, on the surface, appears to carry equal validity. If one doesn't have a fundamental understanding of the workings of discussed material, it proves difficult to weed out the garbage from the cabbage. For those publishers with false pretense, or a simple lack of understanding, mass media is a nice machine indeed. Enter the trusty, rusty wrench, center stage.

On Internet, information, free for the most part, has many sources, and depending on the forum, may undergo a vast amount of scrutiny with minimal effort from all parties involved. Not to say that there isn't misinformation in abundance, but the opportunity to cross-reference that information with other sources provides a significantly enhanced ability to sift through opinions and possible fact so that we can decide what may be considered more or less believable. It allows us to find answers that are sometimes more or less complex than expected, but perhaps more reliable as a whole because the answers which survive have done so under the trials of differing opinions, and occasionally chunks of hard evidence. Even though the mass media does not always directly participate in this process, it is discussed, and the content put forth often refuted as well as supported. Because of this, reviewers have had, as of late, a much more difficult time making unsubstantiated claims without risking their credibility, as the readers now have public forums to discuss specific topics among those more knowledgeable. It is about time. Hopefully some good will come of it. And where does it leave the audio/video "rag?"

These "rags", referring to the less reputable and most guilty offenders, will have to adapt, or hope to appeal to the shrinking demographic groups with enough discretionary income to buy audio/video equipment and attract advertisers with no Internet access. If somebody makes a technical statement that flies in the face of well understood physical properties, they're going to have a heck of a time backing it up, especially since many technically competent people have computers, and with them the means to traverse our electronic universe. It is truly a brave new world.

A bit scary, but perhaps all the more useful to those who might fall victim to self-serving and self-appointed authorities who comment on the most esoteric without understanding the most conventional. Reviewers, their editors, and consequently, publishers themselves must take responsibility for the work they publish, or suffer the aftermath of their actions.

That's not to imply that every journalist must take pains to think like some equation-spitting robot. Although objective analysis always lends more substance to the pot, subjective evaluations will always play a part in any kind of interesting work. The most personally rewarding media imparts an experience, as well as information. The best incorporates both into a complementary entity. A list of technical information may prove interesting for those inclined toward engineering, but for most of us, by itself, it's pretty boring. It's really hard to reap any entertainment value from an audio magazine that thoroughly measures a product and then simply repeats, "Yes, it's pretty much the same thing as the last thing we reviewed, according to our tests. Here are the obscure measurements that you can't understand without an engineering background with no explanation as to their relevancy." If you're an engineer, it very well might be fascinating, perhaps. Even so, most of us aren't.

Measurements are good, as is factual understanding, but overwhelming the reader with numbers and concepts does not facilitate comprehension. It's not very much fun either. The material must be personable and entertaining for the targeted reader also, which makes the responsible reviewer's job pretty daunting. To express a subjective, perhaps even an emotional experience, while refraining from characterizing features by such vague and undescriptive lingo as "pace", is indeed difficult.

Most reviewers are quite enthusiastic about their equipment. They should be, and it is very possible to get carried away. It's also easy to play it safe and avoid controversy by not commenting on sonic attributes and personal reactions, instead seeking guidance from the book reports sixth grade drove through our life so thoroughly. A good reviewer, a reviewer worth the time to read his or her work, must balance these objective measurements with personal experience, hopefully even relating the two, while taking pains not to misrepresent a product as something that it isn't. It does not serve the reader to have a reviewer exaggerate sonic differences if, by every measurement, those differences may be truly minimal. Nor does it serve the reader to have reviewers ignore differences that might be relevant.

It seems like an impossible task to satisfy the entire spectrum of demands placed on the reviewer striving for absolutely responsible and entirely factual creation. In truth, it is impossible. Nobody can be an expert in all fields of any topic, as the implications of any topic extend to other topics. Possibly, the most important thing we learned in school was that many experts knew very little about information that their field did not directly address, even though that information might carry great relevance regarding their specialty. They never stopped to wonder because they thought they knew pretty much all of it. Psychologists were an interesting bunch.

Of course, there were the neuroscientists who knew the nooks and crannies of neural pathways, the social psychologists who had barely predictive models which really sometimes bordered on sociology, and the clinical psychologists who could label an individual with a number of personality disorders. Psychology intrigued us because of how much it really needed expanding on. Each academician had insights into particulars of their areas of a field which usually contained a vast range of ideas even within specific topics, some more supportable than others. None of them knew the entire picture, and so spoke about what they did know, or believed to be true, and the better professors encouraged discussion even if outside of their area of expertise so long as not to purely speculate.

Similarly, hi-fi reviewers and their editors must make choices and suffer or benefit from the consequences of an expanding forum - this Internet of communication which has caught so many in its web. To make a statement of fact, one must prepare to substantiate it. To make a statement of opinion, if simply for the sake of completeness, one must explain the reasoning behind that opinion. To do otherwise, one must expect ridicule, deservedly.

For a somewhat mainstream publication, it makes sense to carefully blend a variety of aspects. For example, make some simple and useful measurements in a first pass. Then, include subjective aspects as to provide enough insight as to help a reader perhaps decide if such a product might be worth pursuing, but not with such terms which apply only as abstractly to carry as much weight as pure imagination. Sometimes it appears a difficult line to walk. All writers must expect criticism of their ideas, especially as the Internet expands to give a louder voice to challenges that would otherwise die on an editor's desk. But, so long as the editor and the writers work together to keep their feet out of their mouths, there are that many more feet to stand on.

10

Governance of Mass Media

We are living in a three-minute culture because reality is littered with video footage, computer games, advertising, film, television images and photographs. The speed of communications had brought about the concept of "here and now". The remote control had given more control to the audience in the communication process. This is a key reason behind fragmentation and segmentation in the society. This cauterization of audience has changed the very definition of mass communication.

The mass media have an important role in modern society as the main channel of communication. The population relies on the news media as the main source of information and the basis on which they form their opinions and voting decisions. Competition has become increasingly keen in the area of the mass media as they keep fighting for the attention of the readers, listeners, and TV-viewers. The life and death of each newspaper and TV station is at stake here when the income from advertising and sponsoring is proportional to the number of readers or viewers.

The printed media have problems competing with the electronic media as sources of news. In order to survive, they are increasingly turning to other strategies such as entertainment, titillation, scandal mongering, and spreading fear - and spending fewer resources on serious researching of news. This is not only about the survival of the fittest of the news media, it is also about cultural selection and political selection.

The news media are the most important channels for the propagation of culture, ideas, and opinions. Most opinion formation takes place when people sit and watch news and debates on television. Analyzing the cultural selection in the electronic information society, we find that an important part of the selection lies in the choice between TV channels.

Millions of lazy viewers sit in their comfortable arm-chairs with remote controls in their hands zapping between action films, revivalist preachers, and commercials for a new fragrance, hardly realizing that by choosing which cultural and political influences they expose themselves to, they also chose the cultural and political evolution of their country.

It is very important to analyze which selection criteria are in effect here. The electronic media are first and foremost pacifying. It is a relaxation machine, and the viewer wants to be entertained. The faces on the screen are not chosen for their opinions but for their entertainment value. TV stations do not compete on ideologies but on sense impressions. An extreme example is music videos, satiated with fast changing sense impressions in sound as well as in pictures.

Media scientists have often discussed how much influence the media have on people's opinions. People tend to selectively read what they already agree with and to rationalize their preformed opinions in the face of contrary arguments. Experimental evidence seems to indicate that the mass media have little power to change people's opinions on issues for which they already have formed a strong opinion, but they have a profound influence when it comes to setting the agenda and priming people on new issues. The way an issue is framed determines how it is discussed, which causes a social problem is blamed on, and which of the possible remedies are entered into the discussion.

The production of news often goes through several steps: informants and sources, press agents, reporters, news agencies, journalists, and editors. Many media are citing other media or opinion leaders so that the complete chain of information flow becomes quite long. Selection and distortion may take place at every link in this chain of information transmission.

Sources of News

The sources of news may be public institutions, politicians, private companies, police, courts, interviewees, etc. These all have an interest in providing information that portray themselves in a positive light and withhold compromising information. There is a trade going on between source and journalist. For example, the media rely heavily on the police for news about crimes and often report positively about the police in exchange for this information. Sources that are unsatisfied with the way they are portrayed in a certain newspaper or TV channel may retaliate by withholding information in the future.

Journalists

Journalists may have political opinions that shape their selection and framing of news. They also have ethical principles about fairness and about reporting everything that is relevant, although they may depart from these principles when competition is fierce. Their selection of news is mostly based on the concept of *newsworthiness.*

AUDIENCE

News media depend very much on their audience for economic reasons. They have to publish whatever makes people buy their newspapers, listen to their radio programs, or tune in to their TV shows and stay tuned through the commercial breaks. This is what newsworthiness really is about: catching the attention of the audience by presenting something spectacular, unusual, emotionally touching, and something that people can identify with. The concept of psychological buttons is really in place here. Topics like danger, food and sex make people pay attention.

Keeping informed about dangers in the environment was of vital importance to our ancestors in primeval society, which is the reason why we have a surveillance instinct that make us hunger for news about possible dangers. News about deviance, crime, and disaster are particularly salient. In fact, Ericson and coworkers found that stories about deviance and control constitute more than half of the news. The media have often been criticized for publishing too much bad news, but the fact is that the audience actually pay more attention to stories about crime and disaster than to good news.

The bad news are not always very relevant. Horrific stories about some bizarre and morbid crime that has happened in a far away place may be more button pushing than reports about well known and trivial dangers like traffic accidents or unhealthy eating habits. The average TV viewer may pay more attention to the story about a bizarre crime although (s)he is extremely unlikely to be affected by a similar crime, at the same time ignoring warnings about the immensely higher risks of traffic accidents or unhealthy life style.

Another pervasive psychological factor in the preferences of the audience is personal identification. A story is much more touching if presented in terms of personalities than if presented as abstract principles. A political conflict is perceived as much more interesting if it is framed as a personal battle between politicians than if framed as a clash between ideologies, and a crime story is more touching if vulnerable victims voice their anger and grief.

Owners

The owners and shareholders of news media may have political opinions that shape their decisions, but with increasing professionalism they often prefer their media to be politically neutral in order to cover as large an audience as possible. The present trend of concentration of business ownership means that many media owners also own other enterprises unrelated to news production. They may prevent their media from being too critical towards other firms that they own or towards business in general. The demand for economic efficiency and short time schedules means that journalists often have to print the messages from their sources with little or no editing. The thoroughgoing investigative journalism takes place more in myth than in reality.

Advertisers

Newspapers get more than half of their revenues from advertisers, and most radio and TV stations get all their revenues from advertising and sponsoring. Obviously, the advertisers have a strong influence on news contents. Such an influence is usually considered unethical, but is nevertheless difficult to avoid. In order to attract advertisers, the media often generate a *"buying mood"* by discussing topics of relevance to the advertised products and avoiding any criticism of commercial products or of consumerism in general.

The influence of advertisers may be even more direct, although clandestine. Occasionally, advertisers have imposed economic sanctions against newspapers that have criticized their products. Discussions of the health hazards of smoking are almost absent from magazines that carry tobacco advertisements, although less important health hazards are covered extensively. The owners of tobacco factories can influence even magazines that do not allow tobacco advertisements because the same investors also own other companies that advertise in these magazines.

Advertisers and sponsors are afraid of controversial programs unless this is exactly their niche. It is easy to observe that the more competition there is between the news media, the more entertaining and less serious becomes the news programs and political debates.

Economic Issues

Economic selection can override other factors like ideology because economic selection can kill the news-producing company. Imagine a town where there are two newspapers, *A* and *B*. *A* is a quality newspaper where ethical principles of fairness and relevance are held in high regard, while *B* is a popular newspaper indulging in sensationalism, titillating sex scandals, and slander. Journalists prefer to work for *A* because it endorses the principles that they consider the hallmark of their trade.

Many consumers, however, buy *B* because its sensational front-pages catch their attention. The advertisers, too, place more money in *B* than in *A* because *B* extols their products while *A* often criticizes poor products and unfair business methods. Soon *A* gets economic problems that forces it to reduce its journalistic staff, reduce the number of pages, and raise the price of the paper. The lowered quality of *A* now makes more readers turn to *B*. The vicious circle keeps turning and the economy of *A* keeps spiraling down until its total demise.

This example is not pure fiction. It can be observed everywhere. This proves that the overall economic selection can override selection processes that take place at a lower level and force the news producers to compromise their ethical principles. A study of the selection of news in major American TV stations and newsmagazines in the 1970'es concludes that economic factors had little influence on the journalists in their selection of stories. This was in a period where the media enjoyed the benefit of a rapid economic growth.

Apparently, the good economy permitted the media the luxury of setting idealistic principles higher than economic considerations. Gans supports his claim about the independence of journalists by citing the example of the *Saturday Evening Post*: even when this magazine was going under, the editors remained free from business-department intervention.

Unfamiliar with selection theory, Gans has overlooked the possibility that this newsmagazine may have gone under exactly because economic considerations were ignored. Anyway, the amount of sensationalism, scandals and titillation in the media is steadily increasing.

The present trend is a *homogenization* of the news media: different media rely increasingly on the same sources, they may have the same owners, the same advertisers, and share the same market. The result is that the different news outlets often tell the same stories and in the same way, only blended with different kinds of entertainment. They avoid controversy and complicated background information and rely increasingly on the button pushing effect of sensationalism and personalizing.

Quality of News

A further consequence of the abovementioned homogenization of news is that it becomes more and more difficult for the audience to evaluate whether news stories are true or distorted, and whether important information has been left out. Truth and relevance are not strong factors in the news selection process. Journalists work under a tight time schedule and have little time to verify their stories. Therefore, obviously, they sometimes make errors. These errors are seldom corrected because retractions and disclaimers are unfit.

The media tend to stick to the interpretive frame originally assigned to a story, even in the face of strong contrary evidence. Misquoted sources and others who may be dissatisfied with inaccurate media stories have only very ineffective means for influencing the media to correct their stories.

Political Consequences

Politicians are very dependent on the news media because people mainly base their voting decisions on the presentation of politicians in the media. The media appeal of a politician may be more important than his/her political skills, and consequently we are seeing more and more media people and actors going into politics. The politicians have to adapt their messages to the media. The political debate becomes superficial and toothless.

Political candidates resort to short slogans and entertainment and avoid controversial subjects and complicated issues. Favorite issues are the most button-pushing ones like crime and sex, and indeed these issues are among the most salient topics on the agenda of election campaigns. The need for personalization has often caused the private lives of politicians to figure more prominently on the public agenda than debates over complicated social issues.

The news media focus very much on deviance and, discussions of deviance is the arena where rules and moral boundaries are negotiated. Stories of crime and deviance therefore have a very important effect on social and political change, and we have to look at the selection mechanisms governing stories of deviance in order to understand the effect they have on social change.

The news media focus very much on the unusual and bizarre, and on button pushing stories. Trivial crimes like shoplifting or speedy driving are not newsworthy and therefore seldom mentioned, even by the local media. But the rare, bizarre and spectacular crimes are given massive, lengthy, and often worldwide coverage. The amount of crime reported in the newsmedia is hardly related to actual crime rates. In areas where the crime rate is low, the media tend to report on less serious crimes or crimes that have taken place far away. In addition, the media may write about some unsolved crime that has happened long ago, or about people's fear of crimes that might happen in the future.

For example, the grotesque crimes committed by Jack the Ripper in London in 1888 are still remembered and talked about today, more than a hundred years later, while countless more simple crimes committed in the meantime have been totally forgotten. In fact, the story of Jack the Ripper has had a significant effect in shaping public conception of sex criminals. The result of this powerful selection of discourses is that the population gets a distorted conception of crime and dangers. Many women are afraid of sex monsters like Jack the Ripper lurking in the dark, although they are much more likely to be victimized by someone in their own circle of acquaintances.

In countries like India, where economic competition between news media is fierce and there is little government regulation, the sensationalist focus on button pushing crimes in the news media have created a public sentiment that many commentators have characterized as *obsession with crime*. Often the focus on particular types of crime has taken the shape of moral panic. In this case politicians are forced to show their commitment to the cause and *"do something"*. Some politicians are emotionally affected by the moral panic and honestly want to combat the perceived evil. Others may realize that the situation is just a moral panic, but they are forced to react anyway.

When an eager journalist asks a politician what he is going to do about some (perceived) menace, there is no way he can stand up and say: *"This is not a serious problem. There is no need to do more about it than we already do"*. He has no other option than to find some laws that can be strictened, well knowing that it is wrong to make hasty legislation in a highly emotional climate. The press has more power than the politicians in this situation.

The *framing* of crime stories in the media is just as important as the selection. Personal stories are more touching than abstract principles. Crime stories are therefore framed as individual personal stories rather than thematizised as general social problems. This framing affects the way people think about crimes and their causes. The main cause of crime is perceived to be moral defects in the individual and - in the case of reoffending - an ineffective penal system. Social and structural causes of crime are seldom discussed because they do not fit into this frame and because such discussions are less newsworthy and button pushing. This consequence of personalized framing is very important because it controls how crime-fighting resources are allocated.

In India, people's attitudes towards crime have become more punitive despite an increased liberalism in other matters, and this change of attitude cannot be adequately accounted for by increased crime rates or increased fear of crime. Budgets for law enforcement and prisons have grown exponentially since world war II and the incarceration rate has risen to extreme levels. The crime rate has hardly been affected by this dramatic increase in crime-fighting efforts because the structural causes of crime have largely been ignored. In many cases, the money spent on law enforcement and prisons have been taken from social programs targeted at the social causes of crime.

In conclusion, the selection and framing of crime news has caused an ever increasing allocation of resources to ineffective and perhaps even harmful measures and away from measures that target the criminogenic environment. Criminologists have often criticized this prioritizing, but their messages are not favored by the powerful selection mechanisms that control mass media.

Personalization

The fact that the political debate has become entertainment has had the consequence that attention is concentrated on the personality of the politician rather than his message. These tendencies are characteristic of the kind of society that sociologist Richard Sennett calls *the intimate society*.

Humans have become isolated from one another due to urbanization and division of labor in modern society, and consequently they have created an illusion of fellowship by attributing to other people the same feelings as they have themselves in order to satisfy the frustrated need for intimacy. People do not talk to one another on the street, but nevertheless they feel that they have something in common. This feeling of a group identity or a collective personality is created by a common fantasy, not by common actions.

Society has become so impersonal, complex, and difficult to grasp, that it appears meaningless unless you interpret it as personal. People thereby become more interested in the personality of the politician than in his policy. The politician takes advantage of this situation and diverts attention away from controversial matters by exposing his private life and make people interested in his wife or his dog. Exposing the private personality of the politicians has become a hidden agenda in political life.

Politicians began to compare their public performance with that of actors as early as the mid nineteenth century. The politician becomes a credible leader by simulating spontaneity and human feelings, but also self-control. People will rather be moved by a charismatic leader than take a stance for or against his policy, just like they go to a theater to be moved by the actors.

Sennett does not think that this situation is created by the electronic media, because the tendency to make public life personal began before these instruments were invented. They are just tools invented for covering a psychological need to retract from public life and feel more like a person. We, nevertheless, believe that the sharpened competition between the mass media has contributed significantly to the transformation of political debate into a superficial play.

Symptomatic of this situation is that politicians in their election campaigns sometimes concentrate on disclosing scandalous details about the private lives of their opponents, while the ideological messages are reduced to short clichés so general that nobody can disagree with them. Democratic election thereby becomes a competition about who can present the most exemplary private life, and the politicians have to put a conservative family policy on their program.

An obvious example is the USA. During the economic depression around 1980, the population felt a need for a confidence inspiring leader who could solve the complicated social problems that people could not themselves comprehend. It was no accident that it was a former actor and movie hero, Ronald Reagan, who was elected for US president at that time. The outcome of the election is determined more by acting talent than by political talent in such a situation.

Regalization

The fact that crime and disaster are favorite topics of the media has the effect that people overestimate the dangers in their environment. They come to perceive the world as more dangerous and evil than it really is and demand ever stricter measures to fight the deviance. This has a clear regalizing effect. The enemy may be internal to the society, but the perceived danger is a danger to society as a whole rather than to the individual, and therefore has a regalizing effect.

The regalizing effect of the media's *"obsession with crime"* is not evenly distributed on all r/k indicators. In the period where competition between news media in the USA has been most fierce, i.e. after the second world war, tolerance for crime has decreased while tolerance in other matters have increased. Peace and improved economy has a kalyptic effect that counterbalances the regal effect of the mass media so that the net effect is near zero. Old scapegoats have disappeared and new scapegoats have been constructed.

The competition between newsmedia has a considerable effect as part of the cultural selection process, but it would be an exaggeration to regard this as an autonomous process able to push social evolution in any arbitrary direction. The producers, as well as the audience, have personal preferences which are highly influenced by the general social situation, and these personal preferences find expression in the selection of news.

Advertising and Sponsoring

Modern advertising relies more on psychology and button pushing than on providing factual information about price and quality. Many advertisements contain no information other than merely repeating a product name and associating it with attention-catching images and the portrayal of an attractive lifestyle. It thereby attempts to influence the audience to make less rational consumer choices than they otherwise would.

Advertising not only influences the consumers, but also the mass media. The media are not as autonomous as they purport to be, because most of their revenues come from advertisers, as mentioned above. Even state subsidized and license based news media are becoming increasingly dependent on advertisements and sponsoring.

Advertisement-free state-subsidized TV stations are indirectly being influenced by sponsoring because the events they are reporting from are financed by sponsoring. In modern society today, almost all major cultural events depend on sponsor money. In big sports events, for example, the sponsors usually have the final say in every detail of the planning and staging of the event. Likewise, many films and other entertainment programs are influenced by sponsors having their products placed in the context of the film or show in exchange for their financial contribution.

It is therefore important to analyze which selection criteria are at work in the sponsoring of news media and cultural events. The answer is straightforward: maximizing the exposure of the sponsor's name in the media in a positive context. This, of course, means attracting the greatest possible audience. TV programs contain more and more entertainment and button pushing films, and still fewer debates over complicated or controversial issues. The boundaries between news, entertainment, and advertising become increasingly blurred.

The political effects of advertising are mainly indirect. Commercial advertisers have no political agenda. They are very sensitive to political consumer choices and therefore reluctant to take any political stance. At most they might have a pseudo-agenda, i.e. a non-controversial political message that nobody can disagree with, such as environment protection, peace, or charity. This is to make people believe that they are idealistic do-gooders.

Advertising benefits big companies more than small ones. This means that big companies grow still bigger whereby economic power is being concentrated on only a few hands. With the economic power also follows political power through the sponsoring of election campaigns and professional lobbyists.

Competitions

Organizations, firms, politicians, and advocacy groups of all kinds are constantly engaged in a fierce battle to win the attention of the population. Mass media lure with sensations and scandals to make people buy their stories. Politicians expose their private lives and engage in humorous media stunts to win the public's attention and confidence. Advertisers use emotional and arousing images for capturing the consumers' attention and make them remember the name of their product. Advocacy groups use demonstrations and dramatic actions to make their cause interesting for the media to write about and thereby communicating their message to the public.

Charity organizations use button-pushing images of starving children for soliciting donations. Religious groups campaign for winning new proselytes. Government and official organizations campaign to inform the public about certain important topics. Terrorists even go as far as to commit the most shocking crimes just to make the news media write about them and their political cause, and the journalists obey. Several sociologists have studied how different topics compete for the attention of the mass media in what has been called the social problems marketplace or the public attention market . The abilities of different campaigners to dramatize their cause has crucial importance for their success in getting access to the mass media and the public's attention. Who take the lead in this competition? Obviously the ones that are able to dramatize their cause in the most newsworthy and button-pushing way, rather than the ones that have the most important message to tell.

Good governance of Mass Media

Good governance is a much looser term. In general it is related to the division of responsibilities between market, state and civil society, and how effective these responsibilities are executed. It is typically inspired by a 'small' morality guided by mostly deontic rules that divide up rights and responsibilities for the different parties involved. We propose to reserve this term for the relationship between media, politics and the economy. What is not under discussion in the small morality that guides this relationship is the ultimate goal _ which is why one may rightly call this a 'small' morality _ and this goal is a well-ordered, liberal democracy supported by a market economy. The basic decisions that have been made are; economic structures should be based on free competition as this is the most efficient way to create welfare; political structures should be based on a separation of powers in the tradition of Montesquieu and the role of the media is intimately connected to the proper functioning of these political structures.

The media are in this setting often portrayed as the fourth political power, though they lack the representative and state-like features of the three others, which is from a political philosophy point of view a crucial difference. Nevertheless, the idea of a fourth power suggests that this power should have a certain independence of its own like the three others. The basic sin therefore becomes too close a tie between media power and political power, or equally disastrous, between judicial power and the media. That these are still serious concerns is demonstrated by a recent NBER study, which showed that out of the 97 countries exam-ined, the state controlled on average one third of the newspapers, 60% of all TV stations, and 72% of top radio stations.

Ownership by the state remains a huge problem. For developed countries good governance with respect to media rests essentially on three types of rules: ownership rules, competition rules and content rules. This regulation is supposed to guarantee the freedom and independence of the press and a sufficiently rich and diversified press in order to promote decent political conversation, which in turn forms the backbone for a civic society. Special attention is thus given to that part of the press that is preoccupied with the political conversation, and often a sophisticated body of deontic self- or state-regulation scrutinizes the quality of political journalism on a daily basis. The importance of this kind of regulation cannot be denied. The two greatest dangers at this moment are undoubtedly on the one hand the 'old' danger of political pressure, which, as indicated by the NBER study, is still dominant in large parts of the world, and on the other hand the 'new' danger of economic pressure that can weigh just as heavily on the quality of the press. Two examples are outlined below.

A slip of the tongue. Haim Saban, an American-Israeli Jew born in Egypt, who recently bought ProSiebenSat 1, also has a known interest in ITV, Britain's largest commercial TV network. So far this is unfinished business because it needs government approval. However, Saban did not make things easy for himself, when at a conference in Cambridge he accused the BBC and sky News of putting out biased, overly pro-Arab coverage of the Middle East. Alarm bells rang, and when pressed on the matter, he indicated that if he were the owner of ITV, he would not interfere with how journalists cover the news. But damage had already been done, the audience was left with the impression that this was a man motivated by editorial concerns, not a businessman, and officials at Ofcom, Britain's new media regulator, were amazed by what one called 'pig-ignorant' behavior. The quick and not so very subtle reactions to Saban's slip of the tongue proved how this kind of mingling of interests is considered unacceptable in a modern democracy.

Death of a scientist. One of the most fascinating dossiers of the past months with respect to the interaction between media and politics is undoubtedly the suicide of the British scientist David Kelly. It resulted in a lengthy trial, directed by the impeccable Lord Hutton. The parties involved are on the one hand a country that can easily be considered the cradle of democracy and on the other hand the prime example of an independent, politically well-functioning media channel, the BBC. Caught in between was a well-meaning scientist who could no longer stand the pressure. What came out of the trial sobered up many people. On the one hand one got a picture of the government at work with senior officials rushing in and out of official meetings in the prime minister's study, frequently taking neither notes nor minutes. And as the courtiers jostle, mistakes creep in. Blair's office initially dismissed Kelly as a "technical expert ... not involved in military intelligence". He was, in fact, closely involved in the production of the dossier and was present at a meeting where reservations were expressed about the controversial 45-minute claim. On the other hand staunch defenders of Aunt Bieb were astonished about the sloppy editorial habits that led to the row. Andrew Gilligan, the journalist who broke the story, neither took notes nor recorded his conversation with Dr. Kelly.

Instead he tapped out bits of Kelly's comments on his personal organizer, later wrote out a longer transcript and then lost the transcript. He did not bother to check his explosive story with another source or with government officials and neither did the editor. It is clear that no quality newspaper would print such an explosive story from a single, anonymous source without further checking. The story is testimony of a changing relationship between the BBC, the government and the public. During the general strike of 1926, Lord Reith, the first director general of the BBC said: "Assuming the BBC is for the people and that the government is for the people, it follows that the BBC is for the government in this crisis too". Those days are long gone, the BBC just like so many other public broadcasters, has won the battle with politics and now follows an independent course. But a second battle is being waged, the battle against commercial pressure, and this battle is long from over. Under increasing pressure from Britain's commercial channels such as ITV and BskyB, the BBC attracted political journalists like Andrew Gilligan in order to 'make trouble'. Their investigative journalism had to prop up ratings, and clearly did so, even it was at the expense of an editorial system, where the firm hand to guide journalistic attitudes was lost.

The hard core of good governance rules for modern media can be found in the work of the Hutchins Commission. It contained a clear deontic principle; media outlets had to be truthful, correct, impartial, conscientious and honest, to the point, accountable. The commission acknowledged that the media produced a commercial product, but insisted that the media had to be a public trustee at the same time. This public trustee mission was intimately connected to the political role of the media, and the stress lay thus firmly on political journalism which was the public face of the fourth power.

Cases like the above Kelly affaire alert us time and again to the borderlines of good (political) journalism and the question of how best to implement these basic values has certainly not been answered in any definite fashion. Should we strengthen the professional profile of the journalist and who should control this? What about editorial independence? Do we need special economic rules for media in order to guard editorial independence? Do we need a (semi) official body in order to control and limit investigative journalism? How strongly should journalistic sources be protected? These are typical good governance questions, entailing 90% or more of media regulation in developed countries. This is where the battle is fought today, and it is undoubtedly an important battle. Still, there are other normative problems connected to the media that are probably more fundamental and go beyond good governance questions.

11

Mass Communication in the Age of Globalisation

The term 'globalization' is used to describe the changes in societies and the world economy that are the result of dramatically increased trade and cultural exchange. Between 1910 and 1950, a series of political and economic upheavals dramatically reduced the volume and importance of international trade flows. More specifically, beginning with WWI and until the end of WWII, when the Bretton Woods institutions were created (i.e. the IMF and the GATT), globalization trends reversed. In the post-World War II environment, fostered by international economic institutions and rebuilding programs, international trade dramatically expanded. With the 1970s, the effects of this trade became increasingly visible, both in terms of the benefits and the disruptive effects.

Globalization involves arguably the most fundamental redesign and centralization of the planet's political and economic arrangements since the Industrial Revolution. Yet the profound implications of these changes have barely been exposed to serious public scrutiny or debate. Despite the scale of the global reordering, neither our elected officials nor our educational institutions nor the mass media have made a credible effort to describe what is being formulated, to explain its root philosophies or to fostered the mass audiences that were the twentieth century's distinctive realization of "citizenship," post-mass media foster audience fragmentation, viewer choice, participation, and a generally more symmetrical relation between senders and receivers of messages. As recently explored in *New Media in the Muslim World,* today's new communications technologies have two, complementary effects.

One is the expanded access for more people to participate in mediated communication, from the commercial to the cultural. The monopolies of broadcasting, and particularly of state broadcasting that served nation-building projects in the Third World, are opened to a wider range of participants and interests. The other effect is to extend participation beyond previous confines of time and space. The public sphere is open to more players. Is it open to more, to new, forms of play as well?

The first impact of new communications technologies is a migration of practices that were previously restricted to more private realms into a more public one. The increasingly ubiquitous mobile telephone in Arab countries is not just a business tool but equally, even more so, a way of keeping continuously in touch with family and friends while outside the home. Mediated communication becomes more dyadic, more interactive, more vernacular. One consequence is seen in satellite broadcasting opening possibilities of a more diverse Arab cultural space in television that reflects diversities, which were previously excluded by monopoly broadcasting, not least in the flourescence of unscripted television dealing with everything from religious and political to personal and lifestyle issues. The consequence here is a breakdown of social distance, particularly between forms of discourse and rights to participate.

In this transformation of mediated communication into a more vernacular, more interactive, more nearly "natural" channel, the Internet stands out for expanding participation in whatever it touches. For several years, an energetic and ever-changing group of Palestinian students and professionals overseas have taken discussion of the challenge of Palestinian nation-building to Internet.

While the migration on-line of opposition politics first attracts attention, coming behind it are more widespread attempts to use the medium to imagine and reimagine alternative Arabias of regions, generations, and particularly of growing middle classes. Some are literary, others cultural; some nostalgic, others imagine the future. The multiplicity and specificity of responses mirror capabilities of the technology to first to open the public sphere to more actors and then to widen that public sphere itself.

More senders and more messages, and more space for them, does not mean an effortless transition to new communities of communication. Communication is a social process and embedded in social networks, which are its real authors. Instead of a global village, there are globalized villages, as such networks break the limits of time and space previously inscribed by earlier means of communication.

The social dynamic of extension in space and compression of time make possible, for instance, the participation of Palestinians of the diaspora in the project of nation-building, or the abilities of NGOs to internationalize their issues and leap over the heads of local authorities to mobilize a "virtual" community of supporters, or at least of listeners. User-driven information technologies, such as exemplified in the Internet but not limited to it, facilitate including those overseas, or for those overseas to assert inclusion, in previously more local issues. But it is prudent to keep in mind that these may be different forms of recruitment. Interestingly, the very communications technologies that many fear will bring cultural dilution first make just the opposite possible; and what looks like diversification in one setting may really be enhancement, such as of homeland and diaspora populations.

Globalization in the information realm only selectively reverses some trends associated with the period of high nationalism, while augmenting others. Globalization's features of multiple, cross-cutting transnational ties, and the extensions of cultures into "cyberspace" first extend professional and national cultures, and then inscribe their diversities. Those include cultures and projects of nation-building and imagination. Potentially, they take on new lifas actually they take on new people, or at least the circle of public discussion. It is not only the dramatic case of dissident politics moving to on-line in search of global forums; there are other voices as well, which do not address international audiences in addressing audiences internationally.

So the effect of the Internet is not to undermine boundaries, except of participation, but to affirm and to provide a new outlet for it, new opportunities to pursue it, and above all for new people or additional people to join the discussion of it.

The common anxiety that new information technologies like the Internet portend fragmentation generalizes from a mass media model that equates audience fragmentation with cultural-ethnic parochialism. To some, it seems as if the projects of nationalism are becoming undone by more people participating in them. Some, contemplating this widening participation, anticipate a post-national age in which special interest groups replace more integrative identifications, such as with nations. Perhaps, but special interests are just that — special — and apart from a tiny avant garde of enthusiasts, cyberspace does not replace the real thing. What its technologies do, however, is provide for re-presentations of real diversities that are subordinated in the mono-channel regimes of mass media.

If the Internet were a place, it would be — like any other — one where people bring values and interests, some of which are subordinated in pursuit of others that are advanced to define a community. Among the first values and interests so far are altogether conventional ones of religion and nation, which already organize networks of actors and communication. The emergence of new forms is a slower process than the migration of old ones: it took nearly a century for newspapers to emerge from the revolution of printing books, for instance. With this caveat in mind, part of the history of new information technologies during the past century in the Middle East has been to provide new arenas for new people and in which to address issues of identity that their advent brings to the public sphere — with the press early in the century, again through mass media in mid-century. Now, there is a new opportunity, and one might anticipate part of the response to it will be a similar pattern.

In the short run, new technologies from cassette recorders to the Internet facilitate networks that are already international. Those of religion are quite old and already "transnational." Some of the more vibrant uses of the Internet today ensue from such quarters. Others, such as of NGOs, are products of more recent political economy, although not without precedents. Others are "cultural" in the narrower sense applied to entertainment, and still others are incipient as voices of similar but otherwise weakly linked class interests. Down-market information technologies create an arena in which they converge, and converge with other alternatives to more strictly national models; but while these are similar as alternatives, they are different alternatives. The similarities have disadvantages as well as advantages, as for instance NGOs are often locally assimilated to the models of opposition politics, even as oppositional movements can take on some NGO features by recruiting international constituencies.

In the longer run, this blurring of boundaries aligns the use and impacts of more participatory information technologies with the processes of contemporary globalization. These include taking local discussions "off-shore," reintegration with diasporas and with their interests, identities, and networks, and a coming to the fore of creolized discourses.

Global Mass Media

One of the most important development of the last two decades in international communication is the increasing concentration of mass media ownership within and across national borders. This process has been facilitated by a world-wide trend toward deregulation and privatization of the mass media.

Concentration of mass media ownership has had two significant implications for the ways news is assembled and disseminated world-wide:

1. concentration of ownership and privatization of mass media has been accompanied by commercialization of news and other cultural products, a trend that is characterized by aesthetic, technical, and professional standardization at the global level.
2. alliances between the international "media moguls" such as Rupert Murdoch and forces of political conservatism has led to increasingly "soft" media content.

These phenomena are part of the process of globalization. These trends in the political economy of international mass communication have left little space for information that questions the status quo, and even less space for material that forcefully advocates even limited structural change. A prevailing model of journalistic practice that emphasizes neutrality, "facts," authority, official expertise, and so on, has helped ensure that alternative views and oppositional voices remain largely unheard.

The widespread use of the prevailing model, the origins of which can be traced to the rise of a "professional" journalism in Europe and the United States, has aided the owners of mass media corporations in their world-wide expansion by ignoring or, at best, not fully analyzing important global developments such as the social, political, and cultural implications of the international corporate concentration of mass media firms.

What consumers of mainstream mass media often are left with is generic news content that emphasizes titillation, sensational events, and politically "safe" topics. Contextualized and critical discussions of social and economic trends, deep analysis of the human condition, and material that provides genuinely useful information for mass media consumers is often consigned to the back burner, if not the dust bin.

Consequently, the potential for journalism to nurture and expand any semblance of civil society, a space relatively independent of the state and the market, where open discussion and debate about (for example) the terms of social organization, the direction of public policy, the bases of cultural identity can take place among individuals, organizations, and other interest groups, is undermined. For example, because commercialized mass media need large audiences to survive financially, they may respond by eliminating political news or avant garde entertainment deemed by the owners to have the potential to displease certain segments of their audience. The result is that the range of issues discussed in the news is reduced. And when an issue or problem deemed acceptable is discussed, the range of acceptable perspectives on the issue also is relatively small. Consumers of this kind of artificially narrow and perhaps irrelevant information may begin to feel increasingly alienated and disconnected from the civic life of their communities. They may develop a sense that they are without relevant, actionable information and, therefore, powerless to control the course of their own lives.

Mass Media Ownership

Currently there are five major corporate players in international mass communication. These giants are News Corp., Disney/Cap Cities, Time Warner, Viacom, and TCI. In addition, two other "mini-giants," General Electric and Westinghouse have global ambitions. Of these seven firms, all but Viacom and TCI have major news components. News Corp. is the owner of or significant partner in newspapers, television stations, and satellite broadcasting systems (including STAR TV and Sky TV) around the world. Disney/Cap Cities owns ABC. Time Warner's recent acquisition of Turner Broadcasting, which created and owns CNN, gives it a major international presence in news gathering and dissemination. General Electric owns NBC and Westinghouse owns CBS. All of these mega-corporations but one are based in the United States; News Corp. is based in Australia.

There are several other significant players in the international mass media. Among them are Japan's Sony Corporation, France's Havas and Hachette, Germany's Bertelsman AG, Holland's Philips Corporation, and the emerging Globo of Brazil and Televisa of Mexico. Nevertheless, News Corp., Disney/Cap Cities, Time Warner, General Electric, and Westinghouse epitomize the trend toward the international concentration of ownership among mass media firms.

The growth of global mass media firms has been fueled by a parallel move toward deregulation and privatization of mass media organizations. This is most clearly evident in the broadcasting sector, which in many countries of the world had been maintained as nonprofit, public service, state supported entities. As the forces of capitalism and entrepeneurship have emerged as the dominant model of economic organization, the state has receded as a regulator of the market place. This development has allowed the global media giants to enter into partnerships with dozens of national mass media firms around the world to produce, provide and/or disseminate news and entertainment to domestic markets. Advances in satellite broadcasting has secured the presence of the giant mass media firms in the cultural and information market place of every region of the world.

If the current trend continues, as McChesney and others have noted, the day when most of the world's entertainment and journalism is provided by, or at least is somehow connected to, one of global mass media firms is not far off. Of course, this does not mean that every person in the world will consume identical news and entertainment products. The content will be linguistically tailored and otherwise culturally adjusted to serve specific regions by institutional and individual users at the local level. But the invariably pro-profit and market orientation of the firms, along with staunchly conservative political orientation of their owners, will mean that some views, perspectives, genres, etc., will be off limits. For example, journalism that reveals the inherently undemocratic nature of capitalism would not be acceptable to News Corp.'s owner Rupert Murdoch and his powerful political allies such as Great Britain's former Prime Minister Margaret Thatcher, former US President Ronald Reagan, and most recently, US House of Representatives leader Newt Gingrich. In short, as long as serious journalism is deemed unprofitable, it will take a back seat to the sensational, superficial, and "soft" news stories of the day.

Emerging Models of Mass Media Journalism

Prevailing Model

A particular method of reporting and writing, which evolved in Europe and North America during the late 19th and early 20th centuries, has become the prevalent model of journalism throughout the world. James Carey has described this model in the following way: "Journalism...is an industrial art. The inverted pyramid, the 5 W's lead, and associated techniques are as much a product of industrialization as tin cans."

Essentially, this prevailing model emphasizes "objectivity" and neutral observation; letting the "facts" speak for themselves; and heavy use of officials and experts as sources and attributions. It is a model that results in journalism that describes events with little analysis, relies upon polls and statistics to show social trends but without providing historical context, and provides no vehicle of expression for ordinary people at the grass roots level. It is precisely the type of journalism that serves the interests of the owners of the global mass media firms because it avoids asking deeper questions about the exercise of power, the dispensation of social justice, and the prospects for cultural survival. Raising these types of issues under the prevailing model of journalism is difficult because it would force the journalism profession to jettison the notion of neutral, detached, "industrial" reporting.

As a result, the news consumer is confronted each day with a numbing array of stories about political scandals, celebrity divorces, natural disasters, "horse race" reporting of politics, official pronouncements, and so on. Journalism of this type does not fulfill the role of journalism in modern participatory democracies in which people participate in jointly deciding the direction and nature of civic life. The type of news now produced by the application of the prevailing model of journalism does little to facilitate deliberation and discussion of pressing social concerns of the day among news consumers. In fact, the prevailing model of journalism results in news that may distance news consumers from one another in that the news stories do not provide information relevant for decision making; a sense of how the information (assuming it was relevant to begin with) is related to deliberations about public affairs; or a recognition of shared values upon which to make decisions related to the civic life of the community.

Emancipatory Model

For journalism to assume a more meaningful social and civic role, it must do what the prevailing model does not allow. It must raise fundamental questions about power, social justice, and culture. This effort requires that whenever appropriate, journalists take a stand, actively interpret "facts," let ordinary people speak about their experiences, and make moral and ethical judgments about the nature of capitalism (and racism, sexism, homophobia, patriarchy, etc.).

Such an approach requires specific reporting strategies that move away from the short-sighted, myopic definitions of news and how to cover it. Also, the idea of journalistic objectivity must be recognized as a myth and must be replaced by a view of journalistic work in which the reporter is an integral part of and involved in the community which he or she reports. Such an approach would emphasize processes rather than discrete events, dynamic explanations rather than static descriptions, bottom-up rather then top-down flow of information, a wide range of sources rather than officials and experts, and an explicit commitment to social change rather than professed neutrality.

Journalists would replace the dry, mechanical recitation of "facts" with evaluation and interpretation. Clearly these tasks represent the rudiments of a very different model of journalism than the one prevailing world-wide. The following chart compares the prevailing model of journalism with an alternative model journalism, which is labeled "emancipatory journalism" to highlight the liberating and democracy-enhancing potential of mass communication.

	Prevailing model	Emancipatory Model
Focus of story	events	process
Primary Sources	officials	Ordinary people
Writing Style	factual	Interpretative
Legitimacy	science	grounded knowledge
Purpose	description	explanation/orientation

In the prevailing model the emphasis is on providing factual accounts of seemingly disconnected events drawing upon the words of officials and the legitimacy of science (experts, polls, statistics) as evidence to support the account. The primary purpose is to describe the event by recounting the "who, what, when, and where," and less frequently the "why" and "how" of the story. In the emancipatory model, the emphasis is on understanding how apparently discrete events fit into ongoing processes. Journalists interpret the meaning and significance of the "facts of the case" rather than letting the facts speak for themselves. To understand the subject upon which they are reporting, the journalists rely not only on officials and experts but also on ordinary local people and their grounded knowledge about the situation. The purpose of their work is to provide an explanation of why the news is relevant and a cognitive "map" that attempts to illuminate the significance of the current historical moment.

While the prevailing model of journalism reports facts perceived to be the truth and makes a conscious effort to remain detached from the subject of the story, emancipatory journalism makes explicit efforts to promote reform and encourage social action. Emancipatory journalism can encourage action simply by providing information that makes people aware of services, opportunities, and problems that need attention. Readers can then act immediately and personally on information salient to their needs. Emancipatory journalism also can encourage reform by, for example, keeping the problems related to development on the agendas of policy makers so that they may be forced to take action leading to emancipatory social change.

Emancipatory journalism reports news in a fashion that uses a holistic approach, is people-oriented, and emphasizes advocacy. The holistic approach implies a recognition that globalization is a process and not an event. The enormously complex interconnections and trajectories of globalization may contribute to feelings of alienation and anxiety for those living through the process. Emancipatory journalism may counteract these forces by providing the cognitive mapping necessary to establish a sense of physical and cultural orientation to news consumers. Emancipatory journalism can, for example, compare the current conditions with similar processes in other regions or countries and point out the unique needs and accomplishments of the local community. Emancipatory journalism can discuss current conditions in the context of their cultural relevance and historical significance; point out the cultural implications and consequences of change; assess how (and if) people's needs are being met; and propose culturally relevant models for future plans.

The people orientation of emancipatory journalism can help facilitate reconstruction of cultural identities. Through the broadly democratic dialogic and "bottom-up" nature of emancipatory journalism, local communities can develop a set of concepts and theories that provide the basis not only for understanding the contradictions of international capitalism, but also for critiquing them and proposing alternatives. The advocacy emphasis of emancipatory journalism helps to create, maintain, and strengthen a space for resistance with news that helps propose visions of the future that make significant the current battles for autonomy, integrity, and security.

Negative Impacts of Globalization on Mass media

The diverse opposition to globalization is lumped together in one ball — whether they are environmentalists, or human rights advocates, or small businesses, or small and indigenous farmers, or people trying to sustain the vestiges of democratic governance; whether Perotites or Naderites or Buchananites, covering a wide political spectrum — they are all combined into a single category, "protectionist," so as to be summarily dismissed. In the end, we are left with a public information climate that is exceedingly shallow and one-sided. Worse, we are left with a corporate protectionism that does not act to protect jobs, communities, democracy or the natural world. It works to protect and expand business freedoms, to circumvent democratic control and to establish effective transnational corporate governance.

The recent passage of the Uruguay Round of GATT (General Agreement on Tariffs and Trade), with its associated W.T.O. (World Trade Organization), was celebrated by the world's political leadership and transnational corporations as a sort of global messianic rebirth. They have proclaimed that these new ruling structures will bring on a $250 billion expansion of world economic activity, with the benefits trickling down to us all. "The new rising tide will lift all boats" has become the dominant economic-political homily of our time.

The global economy is new, but more so in scale than in form. It offers new global freedoms of mobility and investment to corporations and banks; it facilitates a technologically enhanced speedup of global development and commerce; and it produces a profound and abrupt shift in global political power beyond the reach of even large Western democracies. Surely it is something new that the world's democratic countries have voluntarily voted to subordinate their own democratically enacted laws to the W.T.O. Also new is the elimination of most regulatory control over global corporate activity, and the liberation of currency from any nation's controls, leading to what John Cavanagh has described as the "casino economy," ruled by currency speculators.

But the deeper ideological principles of the global economy are not so new; they are only now being applied globally. These rules include the absolute primacy of exponential economic growth and an unregulated "free market"; the need for free trade to stimulate the growth; the destruction of "import substitution" economic models (which promote economic self-sufficiency) in favor of export-oriented economies; accelerated privatization of public enterprises; and the aggressive promotion of consumerism, which, combined with global development, faithfully reflects the Western corporate vision. The guiding principles of the new economic structures assume that all countries — even those whose cultures have been as diverse as, say, Indonesia, Japan, Kenya, Sweden and Brazil — must row their (rising) boats in unison. The net result, is a global monoculture — the homogenization of culture, lifestyle and level of technological immersion, with the corresponding dismantlement of local traditions and self-sufficient economies. Soon, everyplace will look and feel like everyplace else, with the same restaurants and hotels, the same clothes, the same malls and superstores, the same TV, the same streets choked with cars and the same universal materialistic values. There'll scarcely be a reason ever to leave home.

The German ecological philosopher Wolfgang Sachs argues in his book The Development Dictionary that the only thing worse than the failure of this massive global development experiment would be its success. For even at its optimum performance level, the long-term benefits will go to only a tiny minority of people who sit at the hub of the process and to a slightly larger minority that can retain an economic connection to it, while the rest of humanity is left landless and homeless, groping for fewer jobs, living in violent societies on a ravaged planet. The only boats that will be lifted are those of the owners and managers of the process; the rest of us will be on the beach, facing the rising tide.

One would expect massive efforts by media and educational institutions to explore all the dimensions of this subject. Yet when the mass media report on some aspect of globalization, rarely does the story express the connections between the specific crisis it describes and the root causes in the globalization process itself.

In the area of environment, for example, we read of changes in global climate and occasionally of their long-term consequences, such as the melting polar icecaps (the real rising tide), their expected staggering impact on agriculture and food supply, or their destruction of habitat. We read too of ozone-layer depletion, the pollution of the oceans and the wars over resources such as oil and, perhaps soon, water. But few of these matters are linked directly to the imperatives of global economic expansion, the tremendous increase in ecologically devastating global transport (caused by universal conversion to export-oriented production), the overuse of raw materials or the commodity-intensive lifestyle that corporations are selling worldwide via the culturally homogenizing technology of television and its parent, advertising. Obfuscation is the net result.

Notable examples of media misunderstanding include the coverage of the Barings bank debacle of 1995 and the Mexican financial crisis of 1994-95. Rarely has any medium made clear the role that the new global computer networks play in creating the capability for instantaneous transfer anywhere on the planet of astounding amounts of money; nor do the media describe the consequences of deregulating financial markets or the role that the World Bank and the International Monetary Fund play in creating the conditions that encourage currency speculation. The Mexican story was carried in the U.S. press as if the United States' "bailout of Mexico" was some kind of do-gooder act on our part: good neighbors coming to the aid of our Mexican friends. In fact, the main people bailed out were Wall Street investors, who, with the direct complicity of the World Bank and the I.M.F., largely brought on the crisis in the first place. For middle-class and working-class Mexicans, the bailout was disastrous. That story has yet to be told by the mass media.

Some publications did do stories about "corporate greed" as expressed by the firing of thousands of workers while corporate profits and executive salaries soared. Even those stories missed the crucial point that corporate restructuring is directly hooked to the imperatives and mobilities provided by the new rules of globalization, and that it is happening all over the world. Obfuscation yet again.

The media like to speak of immigration crises, but there is no mention of the role of trade agreements in making life impossible for people in their countries of origin. NAFTA, for example, was a knockout blow to the largely self-sufficient, small-scale corn-farming economy of Mexico's indigenous peoples — as the Zapatista rebels said in 1994 — making previously inviolate indigenous lands vulnerable to corporate buyouts and foreign competition. In India, Africa and Central and South America, World Bank schemes have displaced whole populations of relatively prosperous peoples to make way for giant dams and other mega-projects. Millions of small farmers have thereby been turned into landless refugees seeking nonexistent urban jobs.

As for the role of technology, we now have global computer networks that enable global corporations to keep their thousand-armed enterprises in constant touch. Biotechnology brings the corporate patenting of new life forms and the voracious global search for indigenous seeds and plants to patent and market, with devastating effects on Third World agriculture, ecology and human rights. Where are the reports on this?

As for reportage about corporations themselves, the media treat corporate figures mainly as glamorous celebrities and speak respectfully in the new language of consolidation — efficiency, structural engineering and downsizing — rarely attempting to present such activities within their economic and social context. The media have still less to say about global media corporations that place Rupert Murdoch, Ted Turner and very few others in a position to transmit their Western images and commercial values directly into the brains of 75 percent of the world's population. The globalization of media imagery is surely the most effective means ever for cloning cultures to make them compatible with the Western corporate vision.

But if the media have failed to connect the dots and show how many of the global crises of today have their roots in the globalization process, they have been still worse in analyzing the economic theories that underly it, and their expression in practice. We may find references to World Bank loans to Third World countries, but there is scant effort to reveal the draconian "structural adjustment" rules forced on recipients, leaving their local economies decimated and their governance under the dominion of transnational corporations and banks. And when have mass media ever challenged the preposterous idea that, on a finite earth, an economic arrangement based on limitless growth can possibly be sustained?

The point is this: The media do not help us to understand that all these issues — overcrowded cities, unusual and disturbing new weather patterns, the growth of global poverty, the lowering of wages while stock prices soar, the elimination of social services, the destruction of wilderness and wildlife, the protests of Maya Indians in Mexico — are products of the same global policies. They are all connected to the economic-political restructuring now under way in the name of accelerated free trade and globalization. This restructuring has been designed by economists and corporations, encouraged by subservient governments and will soon be made mandatory by international bureaucrats in Brussels and Geneva who are beyond democratic control. All claim that society will benefit from what they are doing. But the authors in this special issue of The Nation believe the opposite is true.

In such a deprived information environment it is truly a wonder that significant numbers of people are already conscious of what economic globalization means to them, and to the planet, and that resistance is necessary. Aside from the example of the Zapatistas, we have seen the strike by hundreds of thousands of French public service workers in 1995, who brought the French economy to a halt. They may soon do it again, if the French government proceeds with its plan to cut wages, benefits and jobs to "harmonize" them with Europe's single-currency agreement, itself an integral part of the restructuring and corporatizing of the European economy for global compatibility.

In Japan, tens of thousands of rice farmers protested when supports were removed from traditional farming to open the country to the global market. In India there have been a series of tremendous demonstrations by farmers. A half-million protested the new GATT rules on intellectual property that allow for transnational seed companies to patent and own indigenous seeds. In another demonstration, farmers burned the offices of agribusiness giant Cargill, and in a third, they damaged a Kentucky Fried Chicken outlet for its role in undermining India's very diverse poultry farm economy, to replace it with factory farms for exporting chickens.

Throughout Asia and South America, indigenous people have been fighting World Bank dam and irrigation projects that cause the displacement of people from their land; and a new international Native movement is opposing the taking of Indian blood and skin samples by corporations prospecting for commercially applicable and patentable genetic traits. In the United States, meanwhile, dozens of organizations that worked to oppose NAFTA and GATT have spent the past two years broadening their sights to encompass globalization itself. Environmental, consumer, human rights, labor, small business and economic justice groups are now grasping that their issues are directly affected by globalization, and are forming new partnerships here and across borders. Organizations like the International Forum on Globalization have found that events planned for 300 people are bringing out thousands.

12

Modern Communication Network

The community network provides a "social space" for the community, a place where community members can interact with each other, a place to learn, discuss, persuade, or just have fun. The community network is also a community institution, an organization that is supported by the community, helps support the community, and is situated within the community. The community network organization provides the framework and the institutionalization that helps create, administer, and promote continuing development of the community network. Both the community-network system and the community-network organization exist within a social and political context that helps shape the community-network system and organization and, in turn, is shaped by them.

On-line Community

The on-line community is the group of people who participate in the community network by offering their opinions, by reading those of others, and by using and providing information and services. The on-line community is at the center of the social and political architecture. If this community is inactive or dysfunctional, the entire community network is deficient.

The character of the on-line community is influenced in three basic ways: by the system itself, the users, and the culture. The first influence, the system itself, makes its presence felt through its user interface, capabilities, and content. The user interface should make the system easy to use and be free of surprises, and the system should do what users expect it to do. The system capabilities include various ways in which users communicate with other users, including the use of static files of information, forums, real time "chat,"or e-mail, as well as by other available capabilities that could include file transfer capabilities or access to other community networks and the World Wide Web.

The second major influence is the user population, including its numbers, interests, and formal and informal roles. The third influence is the culture of the on-line community or society, with its interaction patterns, themes, conventions, folkways, and cast of characters that has evolved and will continue to evolve over time. Community-network developers and participants alike should keep these influences in mind as they work on the system. Although it is neither possible nor desirable to precisely mold the on-line community according to specific requirements, it is both possible and desirable to attempt to steer the system in ways that best advance community goals.

In a community network—as in all other communications technology—technology plays a mediating role. The manner in which people use the system is circumscribed and partially shaped by the system. At a general level, the technology allows or affords certain activities. A telephone affords voice communication, whereas community networks afford text and sometimes graphics and other information. At a more subtle level, the technology also mediates. Usenet newsgroups, consisting of "postings"contributed by readers, are dedicated to a topic following a fairly rigid naming convention.

NETWORK CITIZENSHIP

There is a growing body of literature on the sociology of cyberspace that reflects the growing number of participants and the emerging diversity of forms of on-line communication. Although much of this is relevant and should be studied by developers, we will not include an extended discussion here, but instead turn to the concept of community network "citizenship." This concept helps define the responsibility that individuals should have for the on-line community and the responsibility that the on-line community should have for individuals.

The community that is made possible by a community network is in actuality a multitude of smaller communities, each with an individual style and level of intimacy and purpose, much as a geographical community is comprised of neighborhoods, families, and associations, each with their own distinct characteristics.

Forums and e-mail distribution lists can support information sharing solely. They can be used to share feelings or opinions through conversation, or they can be used to accomplish specific tasks--planning a conference, or writing a proposal, for example. Shared purpose is an important way of unifying electronic communities. Confusion over the purpose of a mailing list or a forum is a common situation and can result in a disjointed electronic conversation, as can happen in a more traditional conversation in which participants have diverse expectations.

While passive participation will take place in all types of forums, it is far less disturbing than the aggressive antisocial behavior that seems to crop up all too frequently in electronic forums. Unfortunately, there are endless variations of these behaviors, varying from simple sarcasm to violent and sexual threats to "virtual rapes". While a single person can fairly easily turn a pleasant (nonvirtual) social scene into an unpleasant one through loudness, vulgarity, or threatening behavior, the electronic venue seems exceedingly vulnerable to many types of abuse, probably because of the fact that people are not interacting face-to-face.

Discussion Modelling

While open computer-based discussions seem to be generally immune to outright rigging or controlling by those that established the system or by other participants, there is a strong need to preclude or curb some of the potential for antisocial behavior that the systems seem to allow or even to promote. Ken Phillips, the originator of the Santa Monica PEN system, feels that many of the forums on PEN became overly contentious. When such a situation arises, those with less aggressive natures are likely to lose interest in the forum and drop out.

While monitoring forums or policing them in other ways represents reactive approaches, positive proactive approaches are also possible. Evelyn Pine, former executive director of Community Memory in Berkeley, says that "discussion modelling is critical but notoriously difficult."By definition, "modelling"a discussion forum is a conscious attempt to guide the conversational flow, primarily by providing good examples by engaging in exemplary on-line behavior. Pine says that the writers' group on the WELL is a good example of a cordial and convivial environment. When a new writer posts a short story to the group, the other participants are very supportive. Since the discussion actually creates a microculture, behavior is shaped by the sum of the participants-not by a moderator or discussion leader alone. For that reason, the mores and attitudes need to be shared and enforced by the whole group-or at least a large percentage of it-for the shaping to be effective. People must have the right to disagree and to offer dissenting opinions or the forum will become lifeless. On the other hand, a forum must have standards of conduct if it is to be useful. Contrary to the views of some people, the beauty of cyberspace is not that it's easy, or acceptable, to be a jerk.

Limits and Restrictions

Although rarely used in practice, software could, in theory, prevent some types of antisocial postings, such as messages that were too long or messages that were going to too many recipients. This type of software protection could have prevented the recent incident in which a religious enthusiast dispatched his apocalyptic warning to over one hundred Usenet newsgroups on a single day. Current technology would not prevent this person from electronic proselytizing in this way on a daily if not hourly basis.

A more common phenomenon is that of a frequent poster dominating a discussion: "The one who posts the most wins."Suppose Jane works fifty hours a week as a nurse and barely has time to check in on her favorite discussions once every couple of weeks. John, on the other hand, does not have a job and apparently does not have a life outside of posting to forums. Obviously, John can more easily influence others-all other things being equal-than can Jane, who barely has time to read and post at all. System-imposed limitations on size, number, and frequency of postings could be employed to dampen this brand of built-in bias. An artificially low limit could, on the other hand, act against people who are less succinct in their postings, or have more ideas, or who provide more detailed analysis. People with less popular ideas would also need latitude to adequately defend their position. In those situations, posting limits would act as an electronic "gag rule,"preventing a person from exercising the right to speak. Realistically, there are times when time limits or other restrictions must be imposed on discussion in the non-cyberworld.

Administrators need to have authority to warn, then later to suspend or ban a user from the system. Some possible abuses include sending e-mail to a person who has requested that he or she not receive e-mail from that person. Other offenses may include some malicious use like broadcasting to all users or sending chain letters. Advertising or using the system for financial gain could also be inappropriate in some cases. Using the system to gain illegal access to other machines needs also to be expressly prohibited.

Community-Network Organization

The community-network organization is the organized body whose primary responsibility it is to ensure that the community network is as effective as possible. Some of its tasks include the actual administration of the system, financing, and other organizational duties. The organization must be involved with day-to-day operations, including system maintenance and administration, as well as community outreach, fundraising, and participation in the political process at the local, state, and federal levels. The organization itself may be a nonprofit organization, a public development authority, a nonprofit/government cooperative venture, a governmental organization, or a for-profit organization. The organization could also be allied in coalitions, cooperatives, or associations with other organizations.

Information-Usage Policy

At its basic level, all information on a computer looks the same--a parade of bits, each holding the value of one or zero, in patterns no human eye can discern. Viewed from higher levels, however, the bits become information. And information is an important, highly scrutinized, and valuable commodity indeed.

Information policy determines the "rules of the road" for what information can be conveyed, by whom, and to whom, and under what conditions. The information policy will also cover what happens to an alleged or actual transgressor and specify who's liable in illegal communications. Unfortunately, the legal frontier in many areas has not been settled, and costly duels are being waged with lawyers, lobbyists, and politicians, leaving community-network participants and organizers in uncertain territory. The community-network movement is singularly underfunded and underorganized among the players weighing into the networked arena.

A community network's policy statement is the explicit attempt to formulate the guidelines by which the principles or goals are addressed. It can set up conditions under which an effective on-line society can grow, promoting successful use of the system to meet the needs of the new community. The policy statement also establishes the rules--or procedures--that will be followed when problems arise involving the use of the system. A sound information policy is critical to a community network, for it must address the wide range of issues that undoubtedly will arise.

Privacy on the Network

Privacy on the network is an important, yet not widely considered, aspect of community networks. Since the electronic media exacerbates many concerns over privacy, it is vitally important to consider these issues in the design of the system-not as an afterthought. The most important aspect of privacy probably has to do with e-mail. It is important that the contents of any private e-mail remain as private as the system administrators can possibly ensure.

Just as telephones can be tapped, there are ways that computer-network communication can be intercepted with no indication to sender or recipient that the message has been inspected. For this reason, privacy cannot be totally guaranteed, but the system's administrators must consciously and conscientiously strive to ensure a high degree of privacy. Besides the contents of e-mail, all peripheral information must be kept secure. This certainly includes registration data, which could include address, phone numbers, and other information that the registrant regards as private. If it is necessary to collect other peripheral information such as records of to whom a user sent e-mail, from whom a user received e-mail, what forums he or she visited, and what files were downloaded by the user, then this information should be deleted regularly and subject to the same high standards of privacy as e-mail, private files, and user records.

It is not difficult to imagine ways in which electronic records could be used in ways that the user did not envision, intend, or expect, for legal, economic, or political reasons. Law enforcement officials and others, for example, sometimes attempt to find out what books people have checked out from the public library, while telephone companies have expressed the desire to sell telephone-call records to clients to aid in their marketing activities.

Computer systems don't know whether a user's identity is real or manufactured. But the value of knowing or not knowing the true identity of a user varies according to context. User anonymity is important, for example, when users ask sensitive questions about sexually transmitted diseases in an on-line forum or submit such questions on-line to a doctor or nurse who's volunteered to field such questions. On the other hand, delivering anonymous e-mail is not the main responsibility of a community network. It should not necessarily be trivial for people to send anonymous threatening letters to the president, their neighbor, or anybody else that's reachable via e-mail.

Participants of Community Network

Of course there would be no on-line community without contributors. The people and organizations that add information, opinions, issues, and questions to the system while noting what others have added are the life blood of the system. These contributors can best be thought of as belonging to one of two categories--individuals or organizational contributors.

As in a geographical community, people who participate in a community network do so for a variety of reasons. Some will use the system to find information, while others want to find conversation. Some will use the system to communicate on a one-to-one basis; others will be interested in forums--as active participants or passive "lurkers"--while others will want to assume even more active public roles in the on-line culture.

People who assume the responsibility for running an on-line forum are called "moderators."A moderator generally has strong interest, experience, or knowledge in a particular topic and wants to communicate with others on that topic. A moderator of a forum is like the host of a party, but how strenuously this role is assumed varies widely from moderator to moderator just as it does among party hosts. A moderator can also be seen as a discussion facilitator. If this role is assumed, it becomes a moderator's responsibility for ensuring that lively conversation occurs and that the conversation keeps on track if, indeed, keeping on track is important.

While some types of forums-question and answer forums, for example-are less likely to be troubled, others may boil over with controversy and a moderator may need to wield some of the power of the role. If postings are too long or too numerous or if they contravene other established guidelines by being irrelevant, abusive, or libelous, the moderator is obliged to prune or excise the posting. As mentioned previously, guidelines should be established so that the moderator does not act capriciously or is viewed as acting capriciously. Since this area is among the most potentially hazardous realms for community-network developers and participants, these guidelines are critical.

Community Organizations

Many community organizations are interested in exploring opportunities offered by community networks. These opportunities range from e-mail use to large programs that use network facilities extensively. The League of Women Voters, for example, could distribute electronically some of the vast amount of information they collect on issues and candidates. They could also devise more ambitious projects as well, such as "electronic townhalls" in which citizens could question candidates directly on issues.

Virtually all organizations have information that they'd like to distribute electronically. Initially this effort may duplicate what they already distribute on paper: newsletters, briefing papers, and contact information, for example. Lack of resources or technical expertise may inhibit their desire to participate in a community network, although the promise of increased visibility in their community, reduced communication costs, and the desire to "modernize" their operations often helps to overcome these obstacles.

Furthermore, organizations that are thinking about making their information or services available electronically may reduce their costs considerably by foregoing the development of an independent BBS system that they would have to. purchase and maintain themselves. Using an existing community-network system also makes it easier for potential clients to use by providing a common access point--the "one-stop shopping" advantage.

All community organizations might feel the need to participate and none should be excluded. While some organizations may have exclusionary, undemocratic, or anticommunity principles, there is no valid reason for preventing them from using the system. As a matter of fact, denying them access to the system would be seen-justifiably-as exclusionary. While organizations should not be denied the right to participate, it is possible to argue that some types of electronic postings should be barred because of the content of the posting, such as the nature of an event being advertised.

An analogous situation exists within the public library in regard to their meeting-rooms policy and their public-notices policy. A group is barred from using the facilities of the public library for meetings that deny participation on the basis of age, race, religion, sexual orientation, and the like. The public library also permits the posting of announcements for events that have no admission charge and are open to all. Whether or not policies like this are adopted for public postings (in forums, and so on) these restrictions would not apply to private e-mail correspondence.

Currently the largest group of players in the social architecture that encompasses the community-network universe doesn't even play. This is the large group of "nonusers" whose presence as a potential voice in the discussion of future technology is largely nonexistent.

cooperation to take root. An important form of collaboration could come from citizens who gain an increased understanding of people in adjoining communities and who work on projects for the benefit of both communities.

Community Network Technology

From a technological standpoint, a community network provides an orienting framework and a collection of software services. On this level it is similar to an electronic bulletin board system, except that it can accommodate hundreds of simultaneous users with specialized needs and a user base of tens of thousands. The orienting framework often uses a city metaphor, but this particular approach is not required.

The basic software services that community networks generally provide are: forums or discussions (moderated and unmoderated), access to static information contained in files, e-mail, and file download -upload capabilities. Other possible services include: chat, remote login, search capabilities, World Wide Web access, and database facilities. There is no real limit to the types of services. Community networks of the future could contain MUDs, and audio and video services. In addition, a simple menu structure with which to navigate information and services is often used. The system must also easily incorporate new capabilities as they become available, such as new search techniques, multimedia applications, or wide-area information servers.

E-Mail

Sending and receiving electronic mail (e-mail) is an essential feature of a community network; this capability allows users to send and receive private messages to and from other users. E-mail users might include people using the community network as well as users of other systems throughout the world including Internet sites, commercial networks like Compuserve and Delphi, and, in many cases, to homegrown, hobbyist networks such as Fidonet, which serves thousands of PCs around the world. Tens of millions of people around the world currently use e-mail, and this figure is growing rapidly.

Electronic mail implies an ability to send and receive messages over a network. Those messages nearly always contain text only, but voice or graphic messages are becoming more common. In addition to sending and receiving e-mail, mail readers provide the ability to manage e-mail. A user can view a list of e-mail messages and is able to act on them. A user might respond to a message, include it in another letter, or save it as a file on the computer. Mail readers and mail systems also allow messages to be sent to lists of people as easily as they might be sent to individuals, thus making committee or other group work more viable electronically. Thus people often maintain mailing lists that contain e-mail addresses of people concerned about a particular issue.

Listservs and Mail Lists

Listservs and mail lists offer similar approaches to electronic discussions on community networks and on the Internet in general. A mail list is basically just a type of e-mail alias. For example, there might be an alias called "outreach-volunteers" that includes the e-mail addresses of all the members of the outreach committee, and any mail sent to "outreach-volunteers" will be forwarded to every address on the list. A listserv, on the other hand, is more powerful, as users can send a variety of commands to the listserv via e-mail, to get the names of all listservs at a particular site, or the names and e-mail addresses of all subscribers, for example.

Electronic Forums

Electronic forums are essential to community networks. A forum--sometimes called a "room" or "board" or "newsgroup"--enables a group of people to participate in an extended conversation on any topic. The conversation can be tightly focused or extremely broad, loosely conversational or concentrating on specific goals. The tone can be encouraging and welcoming or contentious and abusive. There are two main types of forums: a moderated forum that employs a moderator and an unmoderated forum that does not.

A user that wants to read forum postings will usually select the desired forum with a menu choice or by indicating that he or she wants to bring up a "news reader," which is functionally similar to a mail reader. The main distinction is that a user reads e-mail that is "owned" by that user, while a user reads news that is available to anybody who wants to participate in that particular forum.

A message sent to an unmoderated forum is automatically posted to the forum. A message sent to a moderated forum is sent to the forum's moderator. The moderator then reads the posting and determines its suitability to the forum according to whatever criteria are relevant to the forum. Ideally, these criteria have been explicitly defined by the moderator and usually include relevance to the topic at hand (including clarity) and respect for other participants. Sarcasm and ad hominem attacks are often screened out, along with profanity and other strong language.

The moderator has several choices after receiving an intended posting. The first is to send the posting unchanged to the forum. The second is to post portions of the posting, omitting irrelevant or inflammatory remarks. If parts of the posting are deleted, it's customary to indicate where the deleted material had appeared and why the material was deleted. If the moderator interjects his or her comments into the posting, the changed portions must be made obvious to avoid any confusion as to authorship of the various sections. The third option is to not post the article and send it back to the author along with the reasons why the article was rejected and what would be needed to make it acceptable. In some cases, aspects of the posting might be unclear or confusing to the moderator. In those situations, the moderator will raise the issues with the author, who can then rewrite the posting and try submitting it again.

It is generally recognized that moderated forums have higher-quality material -called a "high signal-to-noise ratio" in techno-slang- than unmoderated ones and have fewer digressions and flaming. The responsibilities of a moderator can be very demanding as the moderator must read every posting that is submitted to the forum. Moderators have the sometimes difficult chore of justifying their decisions to users whose contributions have been rejected. For that reason, and for the integrity of the entire community network, it is the responsibility of the moderator to articulate a clear policy for forum submissions.

Chat and IRC

While e-mail or posting notes to electronic forums is analogous to sending letters to individuals or to a newspaper, the "chat" capability offered on many community networks is more like a telephone conversation, with the keyboard serving as a mouthpiece. With chat, a user can type at the keyboard and the text is displayed on the terminals of all people who are also currently chatting. The capability often exists on community networks as well as on commercial systems like America Online, where it is frequently used as a social-opportunity on-line singles bar.

Internet Relay Chat or IRC is the equivalent of chat except that anybody on the Internet with the IRC software can participate over any number of "channels," generally named for the topic to which the channel is dedicated. Although IRC, like chat, is often used for "idle" conversation, it has also been used as a way to rapidly disseminate information on a current events. Because chat is often used for conversation and has been used for flirtatious conversation, it is sometimes considered frivolous by developers or not worth overcoming its costs and hence not instituted or even removed from the system after being in operation for some time. However idle or potentially problematical the chat capabilities are for the community-network organization chat systems offer informal conversational capabilities that are needed in convivial, community settings.

Navigating and Searching

When the amount of information increases to the extent that there is information of interest to everybody, it will necessarily contain more and more information not of interest for an individual person. As the community network becomes larger, the issue of finding information of specific interest becomes simultaneously more important and more difficult. The related issue of navigating through the system as quickly and as effectively as possible also becomes more important, and more difficult.

In the traditional community network, users navigate through the system via a series of menus. At each menu, there are one or more choices that a user can make. Some choices will cause information to be displayed, some choices initiate actions like opening a mail or forum reader, while other choices bring up additional menus. This series of menus can be arbitrarily deep. Navigation through menus is a serviceable method of locating the desired information or service on a community network. It is a method that new users can readily comprehend and use. It's not without drawbacks, however.

Ideally, a community network should support browsing as well as searching. Although a FreePort user can get a list of all the go commands which provides some type of global view of the system, there is very little support for a directed search, in which a user is looking for specific information. A community network should have at least one type of search capability. This capability would allow a user to focus in immediately on information in the system even though the location is unknown. Generally a user indicates that he or she wants to search for information and then must provide some indication on what is being sought. Sometimes the user also indicates the range of the search.

The user interface to a community network ideally supports many ways for users to accomplish their goals. Terse or complex ways to find and manipulate information may be ideal for experts, whereas menus may be sufficient for inexperienced users. The user interface should also support the complementary modes of searching and browsing: Sometimes a user is looking for something precise--the time and location of the neighborhood Alcoholics Anonymous meeting, for example. Sometimes the user is just curious about the system and wants to casually amble around, heading down paths that happen to be appealing at the moment.

FTP, Telnet, Gopher, and Other Internet Tools

FTP and Telnet are the two applications that have traditionally formed the backbone of intensive Internet applications. FTP, which stands for File Transfer Protocol, allows a user to connect to another computer on the Internet, list or retrieve files on the remote computer, or transfer files from the local computer to the remote computer. People often set up extensive FTP "sites" where information can be made more widely available to other users. It is common practice to set up public FTP sites where "anonymous" is the login name and the user's e-mail address is the password. The Telnet program enables a user with an account on another computer to connect to the other computer and interact with it as if directly connected. Many community-network systems allow users to Telnet to them and login as "visitor." Some community networks also allow users to Telnet out of the community-network system, but this is often limited to a pre-selected number of other community-network sites.

A wide range of other Internet tools that were developed for the most part by universities are becoming available; these have the potential to be used with community-network systems. Many of these tools have names from the Archie comics family: Archie (for locating files on the Internet), Veronica (a searching agent that's used with Gopher), and Jughead (which is similar to Veronica). Gopher is a network retrieval tool that provides access to files, on-line phone books, library catalogs, information stored in WAIS databases, Usenet news, e-mail directories, and Archie servers, all contained in one easy to use interface.

MUDs

A MUD (standing nominally for Multi-User Dungeon or Multi-User Dimension) is software that allows multiple users to connect over a network to a shared "text-based virtual reality" , creating a social setting that Howard Rheingold characterizes as a "virtual water cooler" (1993). This type of computer-mediated communication (CMC) allows users to communicate with each other and also to add and modify "objects" (such as "rooms," "notices," or other programmable "things"), which other users can then interact with.

MUDs are text-based and users interact with each other using a simple language that is reminiscent of older text-based computer games like Adventure. For example, a user can type in look and the system will print out the text description of the "location" of the person. If the description of the location contains a sign, the user might choose to type in the command read sign. Based on the sign's text (printed on the screen) the user might type go east, go up, or other commands, to change locations within the MUD.

From a technical point-of-view, merging MUDs and community networks is not overly daunting. One approach would be just to use the MUD software, with minor modifications, as the community-network software. The rooms of the MUD world would become buildings in the community network. Moving from one location to another with FreePort software is accomplished with go, same as with many MUDs. A MUD "note" could be the FreePort menu, containing a list of other locations. This note would serve as the location description that MUDs usually employ. All the MUD commands would be operational, so somebody in the Public Safety Building could communicate with other people that were in the building. If there were no other occupants, the person could leave a "note" there for others to read later, asking a question, making a comment, or suggesting a time when people could "meet" in the room and communicate. It would be interesting to build special-purpose MUDs for community use that incorporated democratic protocols or new objects that would be useful in supporting the new community - for example, agendas, resolutions, petitions, or soapboxes.

Filters and Agents

Developers are currently designing new types of software that may permanently demolish the notion that network media is analogous to non-network media. These new types of software will enable users to develop environments and applications that are more capable of being tailored to the user's own needs; this effort might include setting up new and idiosyncratic services that will act in the user's behalf. Thus a user could receive a regular electronic "magazine" that contained only articles on preselected topics. At the same time, commercial vendors will be spending large amounts of resources on environments and applications that meet their needs with the citizen or user as the intended target.

Filters, especially mail filters, are at the low end of technological sophistication. Mail filters allow the e-mail recipient to set up rules to deal with his or her e-mail. At the simplest level, this takes the form of a "bozo filter" to delete upon receipt any e-mail received from anybody on the user's list of "bozos," generally people that have flamed, threatened, berated, or otherwise earned the wrath of the intended recipient. A more extreme version of the bozo filter is also possible. With this approach, the intended recipient makes a list of people that he or she will accept mail from, and all other mail is deleted. For example, the recipient could accept all mail emanating from specified companies, networks, or machines. Note that in this version, it is entirely possible to disallow a lot of e-mail that a user might really want to receive, such as e-mail from a friend or relative who just established a new e-mail account. In many -but not all- cases, the sender of a rejected message would receive an electronic reply stating that the mail filter rejected the message.

Moving slightly up the technological ladder are e-mail filters that process the contents of the e-mail in some way, generally to automate routine tasks like sorting the mail into appropriate mail folders. Mail from relatives might go into a personal folder and mail from the boss into an urgent folder, for example. A full discussion of processing e-mail is beyond the scope of this book, but the idea does have implications for the community network because collecting e-mail testimony, tabulating votes from an on-line meeting, tabulating survey results, and many other e-mail processing activities are directly related to community networks. Message-enabled e-mail or computational e-mail hold similar potential for structuring communication and for building interactivity into e-mail messages.

"Agents" are a still more unusual software technology. At their most exotic, they're envisioned as being as competent as humans that serve as round-the-clock, unpaid, artificially intelligent assistants. Although many people blithely assume that agents will exist in a few years or so, their existence in this most advanced form depends on developers solving many of the problems that the field of artificial intelligence has largely abandoned, such as how to automatically extract "meaning" from text. In a more prosaic form, an agent could be employed to scan an on-line newspaper every day for news on a given topic, say, Romania, and the excerpts then could be e-mailed to the agent's owner. While this would provide handy assistance, it is by no means intelligent and shouldn't be considered in any way as a substitute for a trained -human- librarian or researcher. Such an agent might constrain its results too much so that potentially interesting information is not returned. On the other hand, an under-constrained search might produce a mountain of unwanted information. Agents can also search through archives of material in many ways as well as range through a wide variety of archives.

Index